JOURNAL OF A HOLIDAY MAKER

From North London to South Africa and Zimbabwe

There is an Elephant in our Camp;

a Hippo in the Water and a Monkey Stealing Bread.

SHIRLEY WATSON

For Mum and Nana Thomas.

To My late Mother, Mrs Reverend Elsie Watson.

One of the first women of colour to be ordained into the Church of England.

Mum thank you.

CONTENTS

ACKNOWLEDGMENTS

Mrs Shirla Philogene OBE, for all her patience, kindness and love.

Ms V.R. Watson, for reading and re reading all my drafts.

Duro Adebayo, for his sweetness and for being my son.

John, for putting up with me on this life changing holiday.

PROLOGUE

This is a book of memories of travelling to Africa for the first time.

The political tensions of the two countries I visited: South Africa and Zimbabwe in Southern Africa forms the backdrop for this book.

South Africa, where separation of the Races was enshrined in law, began with the East India Trading Company who took up a post in South Africa to supply passing ships with fresh fruits and vegetable on a temporary plan. The Settlers (Dutch) soon began to establish themselves by building houses, which upset the natives. The Company sort to keep the peace by limiting the amount of land the Settlers could use but this upset the Settlers. During the Napoleonic wars the British took the post as a naval station. The Settlers found rule under the British worse than the East India Trading Company and in 1914 the South African National Party was formed by James Barry Munnik Hertzog to protect the interests of the Settlers. The Settlers, although only representing 12% of the population, (but they owned 86.3% of the land) the South African National Party, came to power in May 1948 with a wave of rural support. The party under Prime Minister Dr Daniel F. Malan began the process of establishing Apartheid.

The belief of Apartheid is that Whites must be separated from non-whites (jobs, schools, railway station, beaches, park benches, public toilets and marriages must not happen between the races). For this to happen there has to be strict controls; therefore all non-whites men must carry passes (the Pass Law), which must be stamped to allow a non-white to remain in a white area for longer than seventy-two hours. The pass law was later extended to include women, for which the penalty for violation was thirty days imprisonment.

The only comparison I could find was that of Alabama in the US where the Races even had different days on which to shop. The four main categories were: Whites (European), Blacks (African native), Indian and Asian (Indian and Pakistani), Coloureds (any mix of the mentioned categories). The Apartheid regime not only separated Whites from non-whites, it also separated Blacks from the other races: Whites earned eight times more than Blacks and Coloureds earned three times more than Blacks but half of the earnings of Whites.

Below is a citation from an Essay entitled 'Our Land, Our Life, Our Future' on the Web Site: www.sahistory.org.

The nationalists, having come to power on a strong rural vote, embarked on a process of systematically eliminating the few African tenants that remained in White farming districts and of transforming labour tenancy into wage labour.

Farmers, who in the 1930s and early 1940s were desperate for unlimited supplies of labour, now began to view labour tenancy itself as economically backward. The consensus was that if agriculture was to modernise, labour tenancy had to be abolished.

These calls by White agriculture were not ignored. The 1964 Bantu Laws Amendment Act, which repealed the 1932 Native Service Contract Act, and amended the tenancy provisions in the 1936 Land Act, dealt the final blow to labour tenancy. Over the decades that followed labour tenancy was progressively eliminated. Evictions were carried out by farmers themselves or by officials of the Bantu Administration.

"We then heard that the six-month system had been abolished and we had to work for the farmer all year round in order to continue living on our land. We were quite agreeable to this but said that our children would starve if we had to live on the low wages that we were getting on the farm for the whole twelve months. If the farmer would pay us more, we would gladly stay on the farm where we were happy. The farmer refused. The Bantu Administration Department told us if we were unwilling to work for the whole twelve months we would have to go to the location." – Dombi Khumalo, labour tenant.

In 1961 South Africa became a Republic and separated itself from Britain. The increasing resistance, the growing number of Black Trade Union activists and the realization of the economic power of the individual (by withholding their labour thus reducing profits) resulted in ever increasing brutality inflicted by the government in an effort to maintain control; which accumulated in the 'Sharpsville massacre' of March 1960 in an anti-Pass march consisting of 300 people. Approximately 69 people including school children lost their lives when police opened fire.

The growing desperation of the government showed itself by the increasing declarations of 'States of Emergencies' 'media station close downs' and 'media blackouts'; it even became illegal to report or show pictures of SOWETO Township.

By the 1980s and 90s the international gaze was becoming more focused on South Africa and at home in Britain the youth had turned its back on the then Prime Minister, Mrs Thatcher's, adamant refusal to instil economic sanctions on South Africa; and instead had galvanized their efforts to support the release of Nelson Mandela from Robben Island Prison.

Nelson Mandela was released from prison in 1990, after serving twenty-seven years on political charges; and now the first free multi-racial elections were due to take place, in the April, four years after his release.

In Zimbabwe President Mugabe was becoming less in favour with the UK government. The history and the complexities of Zimbabwean politics can be summarised:

During the late nineteenth century the Europeans began to move from the South and settle in Rhodesia; before this Rhodesia was used by the Europeans for game, hunting and trading in its natural resources. The natives Ndebele people from the Matebele Kingdom rose up, against what was happening, but was easily and swiftly defeated.

The Land Apportionment Act restricting Africans to own land forced many into working for a wage. This generated a growing opposition to Colonial Rule and led to the formation of two of Zimbabwe's political parties: the Zimbabwe African People's Union (ZAPU) and the Zimbabwe African National Union (ZANU). The election of 1964 was won by Ian Smith, who, a year later asked and was refused

Independence from Britain. Ian Smith decided to take independence from Britain anyway, which caused almost a decade of guerrilla warfare.

Britain eventually agreed independence and asked for (British educated) Robert Mugabe to supervise elections; which he won in 1980 with his ZANU party and invited ZAPU's Joshua Nkomo to jointly govern. However, after only two years President Mugabe sacked Mr Nkomo with the accusation of plotting to overthrow the government and five years later becomes the Executive President by changing the constitution.

In 1991 the Common Wealth adopts the Harare Declaration, which, commits to a vision of international peace, security, democracy, equal rights and freedom of the individual. However, there was a growing unrest in Zimbabwe of no positive economic changes being felt by the majority population ten years after Ian Smith.

The year was 1994.

The narrative and observations are from my perspective i.e. that of an Outsider who has been exposed to the attitudes and norms of ordinary people going about their everyday business of living and who have been shaped by the political environment that they have found themselves.

It has also enabled me to glimpse into the unconscious part of what makes us people; the part of our mind that reacts automatically without analysis or wilful suppression; the part that instinctively reaches for extra clothes when the weather changes to cold, intuitively want to protect our young, eat when we are hungry or rub our eye when there is something in it.

I was coming from Britain and enjoyed *freedom* (to marry, live, work, travel, pray, shop, without restrictions) and *democracy* (vote without fear, raise issues in Parliament through my MP and could enter politics should I choose). It is from this point of view and my life experiences, which, forms the Journal of a Holiday Maker.

The temporary status of 'just passing through' brings an enormous sense of freedom to the individual when you are in a country but not part of the country. As a 'Holiday Maker' I was granted a 'freedom' to see people and make comparisons of situations that may have otherwise been missed or not observed as acutely by the natives who (apart from not having anything to compare against) may accept things as the norm.

We left our home in North London, UK on 29 December 1993 and returned on 19 January 1994 all of twenty-two days later. The book chronologically charts events, feelings, adventures and encounters that filled those twenty-two glorious days.

We had a truly wonderful and fun time; first arriving in Johannesburg traveling to Zimbabwe then returning to South Africa via Johannesburg before going on to Cape Town and finally flying out from Johannesburg to home.

We still reminisce about this period in our lives and hope that you too will enjoy reading:

The Journal of a Holiday Maker: From North London to South Africa and Zimbabwe.

I marvel at the human spirit and its quest for survival.

SECTION ONE

NORTH LONDON

Two Weeks Before Departure

29 December 1993

This is us

A three week holiday touring Southern Africa was the icing on the cake and marked our fourth year of being together!

Time had flown by so quickly since our first date; time passing rapidly is one of the sayings of those with old eyes that is often rebuffed by the young; until they have become the ones with old eyes.

I was working at a large teaching hospital in London as a Ward Sister and Sharif as an IT Consultant in the City of London. He already had his house, so, when the time was right it made sense to combine our resources and move in together.

I moved onto a street where age or skin colour was not an issue; everybody knew each other and had a comment or two to make about everyone else. In the summer evenings the street would buzz with laughter followed by the men slapping their thighs in recognition that a 'sweet' joke had just been told. In the mornings audible 'hellos' from the young to the old as children ran the gauntlet of people to whom they must greet and the dropping of something, anything, then the inevitable call of 'wait for me!' while the 'something' was retrieved from the ground, or the more usual 'don't wait then!' as they made their way to school.

The high street was at the bottom of our road. Our road formed the shape of a capital 'Y' with the left '\' forming a cul-de-sac or a dead end with only six houses. Those who lived on this limb felt that they were more 'posh' than the rest of us who lived on the other side of the medium length inner city residential road. I only know this because Mrs Wilson had argued with a lady from there and the lady had said that she, Mrs Wilson, was as 'common as the rest of them on that side'.

The lady, who had left the road many years ago, had unwittingly given Mrs Wilson 'a way in to the lives of all new residents' by her retelling this little tale and so was able to be the first to 'befriend' any new household. Mrs Wilson knew, long before anyone else, the people's names, how many children, which school they attended, who worked and who did not. The new residents and I include myself in that; just saw Mrs Wilson as a friendly older lady making chit-chat and if it had stopped there it would have been true.

The right side of the 'Y' curved back in on itself almost in the shape of a 'C' and formed the 'T' junction with the adjoining road crossing the top of the 'T'. It was this adjoining road that if I turned right, would take me back to the high street.

The high street on a Saturday was a hive of activities; it was a meeting place for young and old. There were several hairdressers and barber shops, an estate agent, fruit & veg shops, fried chicken shops, several take away, pubs, newsagent, cash and carry, Italian patisserie, travel agent, a dry cleaner, fish mongers, butchers, a book shop and even an indoor market.

In places such as where we lived, it is inevitable that characters emerged and here was no exception. These characters are painted vividly across my mind:

Mark and Mary, owners of a fruit and vegetable stall lived at number 32. He had inherited the stall from his father and now was forced to sell as they sort an easier life for themselves and their two Alsatians.

Mary was what you would call 'chatty' but had a heart of gold and would do anything for anyone. She had eyes like a hawk, and a well-developed voice from years spent calling to customers from the mantel of her stall. What also did not help her cause was her hearing, which, was not as sharp as it used to be. Mary would greet you from the end of the street where she stood and first clapped eyes on you even if you were at the other end of the street; rather than doing what was customary of waiting until both parties were close to each other for such exchanges to take place. I can only imagine that Mary viewed the large space between her and the individual as a 'waste of good talking time' and so would conduct her conversation (embarrassing as it could be to the other party) with easy innocence and a smile often not reciprocated.

The conversation may involve asking the occasional questions and or confirming anything else as and when it came to her mind. This annoyed poor Alice Thomas, a quiet God-fearing Jamaican lady who was no longer 'too good on my legs' had just returned from an extended holiday in her home country.

She had, not so long ago, experienced such an encounter with Mary and I believed had vowed to herself that it would never happen again.

It was a fine summer's day in North London; Alice had been out shopping and was returning home when she noticed Mary; who, she believed, did not see her because:

1. Mary and Pat were involved in a juicy conversation at Pat's gate at number 26 and

2. Mary had her back turned; this was for extra security so no one could lip-read as they approached.

The truth was that there would be no need to lip-read, as the approaching person would be able to hear Mary, even in her whispered tone, from a few feet away.

Alice seizing the opportunity to avoid Mary, quickly turned in the opposite direction of her travels and leaving herself little option but to walk away from her destination thus giving up all possibility of having to pass Mary and Pat before arriving at her own home at number 38; by which time (she had quickly calculated) they would be long gone. However, in order to achieve her impromptu plan, Alice would be duty bound to add an extra half-mile to her journey taking her around the block and eventually arriving at her number 38.

Alice set out on her unexpected detour anticipating to hear Mary hollering her name and because of this could not fully relax until she had turned the corner and re-entered the high street from which she had just come.

Alice set to walking as briskly as her legs would take her arriving at number 38 tired and flustered; she placed her keys into her door and fell into a heap onto her newly carpeted hall.

Mary and Patricia still deep in conversation and not being any the wiser of the drama they had caused to poor Alice, who, was laid up in bed for the next three days being nursed by her daughter who had called on me for the occasional nursing advice.

Number 89 was considered the 'drug' house and all sorts of people could be seen entering and exiting during any of the twenty-four hours in the day. All decent folks avoided this house!

A multi occupancy where the tenants had no idea of whom else shared their property with them, was number 110. Here it was rumoured that a man dressed in overalls and a donkey jacket, casually walked through the front door which was left wide open and marched out again having gone from room to room, with a bag collecting the occupants' properties before leaving the same way he entered.

Then there was Eric. Eric lived with his parents Bob and Jean Maynard at number 105 and considered himself 'a Ladies Man' but being all of '4ft 7 and three quarter inches', as he would gladly tell anyone and everyone at the drop of a hat and having the well-developed habit of 'digging for gold' and eating it; the ladies did not consider Eric their man.

Away from the high street but still in walking distance was a sports centre. In this space several community events took place:

On election days it formed a polling station for the local residents; on Sundays it became a church for at least two different religious beliefs; during the week it retained its original purpose of library, swimming pool, sauna, steam room and gymnasium and hosting different community exhibitions in its foyer.

So this was where I now called home and with all its faults and characters this is how I liked it.

No Passport and Somewhere to go

Exactly two weeks before our anticipated venture to South Africa, a house burglary took place it was our house that was burgled and what's more both our passports were stolen.

We arrived back from work (as we would meet each other at Kings Cross underground station and travel home together) and placed my key in the door; today of all days the key, which, normally opened the front door without any problems has decided not to work.

I turned to Sharif and told him that my key did not work; he stepped forward and tried to open the door with his key but that did not work either! He quickly came to the conclusion that we had been burgled.

Our priority now was how to regain entry into our house. Sharif went around the back entrance and managed to break a window and was then able to open the front door to let me into the house via the front door.

Once inside the house there was no telling if s/he was still inside.

We called the police.

We walked around the house together and went into every room, making sure we did not disturb anything, until the police arrived.

I could sense the urgency in which the thief sped through the house: grabbing then dropping pieces of the loot as he made a rapid exit.

The police, a baby-faced polite young man, duly came and told us that there was hardly any chance of getting the items back but we could check the local second-hand shops or car boot sales; they will take finger prints and issue a number for our insurance claim.

The thief was either generous to a fault, had very poor eye sight or it did not fit with his plans to travel abroad at the time or didn't know anyone willing to buy the tickets because although stored together with the passports, both our tickets were left intact.

We now had two weeks to replace our passports in a process, which would ordinarily take four.

After reorganizing ourselves to enable us to arrive at Petty France in the early hours and pay over the odds (but at the time worth every penny) to be able to walk away with a brand new passport in our hands; only then were we able to breathe a deep relief in a way felt by many but only truly known by those who had gone through a similar 'close-yet-so-far-away' kind of experience and come out the other end smiling.

So both relieved and with a deep lung full of air, (not passing up the association with life itself) we were able to continue moving forward in our lives, with our plans of our dream holiday together, to explore Southern Africa with South Africa being our starting point.

South Africa! Why?

Still filled with apprehension:

I wonder at the type of person who voluntarily yes willingly, without family ties and with freedom to act, travels into a political regime renowned all over the world for its brutality, mentality of superiority and the brutal killing of school children?

The answer is people like us; we would!

However, it was not an easy decision nor was it taken light-heartedly. We battled with and talked through our decision at every opportunity leading up to our leaving the UK and our arrival.

We spoke to each other, to friends both separately and together, we spoke with South Africans and silently we spoke with our individual conscience in the dark of the night when no one else could hear, comment or throw scorn on our inner most thoughts.

In our minds questions of whether we were supporting such a regime by our very presence in the country tormented us.

Or…

Were we just plain and simply naive 'Travellers' wanting that 'one last adventure-adrenaline-rush'?

I hear myself saying in justification that:

'Many people travel to South Africa and they returned safely.'

In fact at the time, despite the talk of boycotts and sanctions, many British entrepreneurs continued to quietly open new or expand old businesses in South Africa. But with some the very nature of what they did, as sports and entertainment personalities, could not do their jobs quietly and therefore were shunned by many for daring to venture to South Africa to continue sharing their talent with the world and in doing so earn themselves a handsome living.

'Yes, that maybe so BUT most were not black skinned,' he replied.

Wishing to continue with the discussion, I pointed out that there might be a greater manipulation happening:

For discouraging educated people of colour, who may have ideas and experiences (that would be considered by the regime as being) 'above their station', would indeed prove too destabilizing and upsetting for such a regime if too many of 'those-types' of people entered South Africa.

However, and at the same time the regime quietly encourages 'like-minded people' to come and enjoy the better lifestyle and all that South Africa had to offer, and in doing so strengthened the regime with their presence.

Sharif went to school with Gary but they had each moved in separate directions only to be reunited in London years later. Sharif had decided to make full use of a rare sunny March day in England by sorting out the house and removing all his unwanted items to the local recycling yard. He duly loaded up the car and packed as many items in it as he could and set off to dispose of them once and for all.

On arrival at the yard he noticed a person with a distinct *walk* approaching him. The person was walking as though one hip was just slightly higher than the other therefore tilting his body off-balance so the walker naturally leaned to one side (in this case it was to the left). This **was** Gary and after exchanging contact details and a flutter of brief phone calls exchanging between them everything fell silent. On deciding that we would go to South Africa, Sharif had tentatively tried several numbers before being able to speak with Gary and 'catch up'.

At the age of fourteen or fifteen and growing up on a farm in Yorkshire, Sharif had invited Gary to help out, so that they could both earn some pocket money for the long summer holidays ahead of them.

Gary was pleased to be offered such an opportunity and accepted quite readily. However, Gary, not being as familiar with farm life and its inhabitants, had decided not to heed the advice of the wise and 'did his own thing' despite repeated warnings of the dangers that laid (not so well hidden) in a place such as his new surroundings of the farm.

In the hospital bed Gary laid still underneath the white cotton sheet. His broken leg, now secured with a heavy weight hanging over the bottom end of his bed and attached by strong ropes, which the nurses kept referring to as 'traction' and the doctor repeating the phrase, 'He was lucky she kicked him so lightly, very lucky indeed'.

It was a full two days before Gary was able to retell the story of what really happened after Mr Sutcliffe had asked him to fetch the full milk churns from the cow shed forgetting that Jemima (his best milk producing cow) was still inside nursing her young.

Unfortunately and unknowingly Gary had chosen not to (just) collect the churn and return to Mr Sutcliffe (that was the unfortunate bit); but instead had approached Jemima too quietly (he thought not to disturb her intimate moment with her calf); and from behind – something most would know not to do.

I still believe that Gary must have stepped on something like a dried branch or done something to startle Jemima because the next thing Gary recalled was that he was on the floor hollering in pain after hearing a firm stamp from Jemima's back hoof. Gary had said that Jemima hardly moved.

Mr Sutcliffe, a man who shunned the town and the town folks, had panicked and placed Gary on his tractor to take him into the hospital; once on the main road, the tractor being slow and Gary hollering in pain attracted the attention of a local doctor who happened to be on his home visit calls. It was he who called for an ambulance and got Gary to hospital safely and in good time.

Gary's leg eventually healed following several infections and further operations; but alas children can be cruel and as he made his way around school; he was forever known as an instrument for holding clothes on the washing line followed by the word 'leg'.

Gary was eager to get away from those children and rebuild his confidence by getting a job (something that none of the others had, since, they were still at 'only' college).

Gary was not so concerned with the type of job or the prospects the job offered; but that he was considered to be 'a man' earning a wage and not like those 'still children' at college.

When 'the children' started leaving college and getting a different sort of job than Gary; he thought that he would move to London and leave them to their future.

The only job open to Gary, at the time, was a job at the local Recycling Centre sorting household waste (his father's friend had worked there and recommended him for the job).

With his life in the UK going nowhere fast; Gary had made, what he felt at the time was, a tough decision to turn his back on Britain, leave his friends and family behind and head to South Africa.

In South Africa and with a British passport; Gary was employed in a position of authority in-charge of a distribution warehouse; he was able to purchase a gated house with a pool and employed staff to manage his home to enable him more time to 'enjoy life'; he was welcomed into an expat community and naturally embrace his new social calendar. He was now able to fly back and forth between the UK and South Africa.

South Africa had given him a lifestyle that, had he remained in the UK, he could only dream of and access to people of a certain elite. As expected Gary could not envisage the UK ever being his permanent home again.

So the country worked for Gary.

In 1990 Nelson Rolihlaha Mandela was released from, Robben Island Prison where he had been held for twenty-seven years on political charges; and now in three short months the first elections would be held that would include all South African nationals for the first time ever!

The climate for change, the possibilities it gave, the anticipation of a better and freer South Africa filled, in fact coated, the air and with each breath you became infected with this same optimism!

The South Africans embraced the concept of a 'rebirth' of their beloved South Africa. With their visions of South Africa rising up once again from the ground (of exclusions and sanctions) and taking up its position at the global table once more; as it would now, irrespective of skin colour, offer opportunities to everyone.

I saw the chance for South Africa to place, firmly in the past, all the brutality that had gone before.

I remained optimistic but secretly questioned if this vision could be made real after decades of cultivating such a culture?

A mother knows the pain to be endured in order to have her new baby who, symbolically and in this scenario, may represent:

'Hope',

'The future',

'An opportunity for change' and 'The unity of the Races'.

Sharif and I felt compelled to witness and taste the

air of optimism for a country on the cusp of such monumental transformation;

We had to be there!

SECTION TWO

30 DECEMBER-3 JANUARY 1994

Johannesburg South Africa

Up! Up and Away

Flight SN6 left Heathrow on time, which, came as a bit of a surprise to us; maybe due to previous unrest at airports or an inbuilt cynical reflection on the low expectations of flights leaving on time.

The turbulence of the plane was apparent as soon as we began our journey across the channel to Brussels. In Brussels everything inside the airport looked pristine. To the right of where we were standing were shops displaying the designer names of Chanel, Armani, Yves St. Laurent and so forth and to the left was Gate 36; we entered Gate 36 on an exit flight number 551 direct to Johannesburg.

On the plane journey the new accents were all around us and we felt conscious of being the only two black people on a South African Airways flight of at least 400 people.

It was too late now to even consider turning back, so, we continued with the thoughts uppermost in our hearts and minds of a must-see new dawn of the born-again South Africa.

We ventured on, to our first leg of our Southern African experience, flying into Johannesburg twelve hours, after we last saw our home in North London on 29 December, to arriving at 07:45 on 30 December 1993.

I learnt that Johannesburg is the largest city in South Africa and had several different names by which to be called such as: Joni, Joeys, JHB, Joburg, Jozi; and its Afrikaans Jo'henesboerx. I quite liked 'Joburg'.

Having disembarked into the Johannesburg International Airport, with palpable levels of anxiety and excitement in equal measure, we were ushered systematically through the airport in a manner common to any other port around the world (I am not sure what we were expecting).

Tired but relieved of having completed a safe and uneventful flight we were now standing under the full gaze of an Immigration Official, who turned his head from left to right in quick succession and switching gazes from passport to the real-life face in front of him; in a voice audible only to those in close proximity, he uttered, 'okay' and followed this affirmation with a small firm nod signifying we were free to go.

We survived passport control and even though to my knowledge there were no reasons to anticipate that there would be problems; it was a relief never the less, when there were none and we both came through.

We headed towards the green sign that read

'Nothing to Declare'.

And so we had officially entered South Africa!

Still within the compounds of the airport and on high alert for evidence of the unjust treatment we hear about whenever 'South Africa' is mentioned and now has become two words synonymous with unfair treatment of its host population; my gaze fell on a hunched figure on the floor of the airport.

As the image I had fixed my gaze on became clearer of being that of a lone black woman on all fours, knees bent and both arms out stretched and in contact with the floor. Her stiffened left arm with elbow locked for balancing clasped a mop-head in her right gloveless-hand and in order to direct the mop for cleaning she extended her right arm in replacement of where the mop handle ought to have been. With her lips moving in way of some familiar song she slowly moved her head to come to rest wearily on her left shoulder; then in the same slow monotonous exasperated way the head moved to her right and so she went on cleaning.

Witnessing the lady's bare hands where the long handle ought to have been, filled me with dread of what else was to come. Glancing around the huge space of the airport, made me rapidly absorb the vastness of such a futile task that strewed its endless self in front of the woman; my stomach sank for her.

The lady, with her tight head wrap and sweat beads falling from her forehead, sat back on her bent legs curled under her and using both hands to squeeze the mop of excessive dirt and water slapped it down onto the space overlapping the area she had last scrubbed, of god-knows-what: she then began to rubbed the floor with vigour and all her might; before returning the mop to the bucket. Repeating the process all over again but this time in even greyer and murkier water than before, she inched her body forward in recognition of her slow and arduous progress.

With the thousands of pairs of shoes, boots and sandals, passing her trampling and marching as individuals but in unison, it dawned on me and made me feel sad that they did not see her, they were aware of a 'being' obstructing their path but they truly did not really see her. She was in fact invisible.

Those passing by her, I am sure, appreciated the standard of cleanliness of the airport floor and managed to negotiate with some degree of skill and precision the pull luggage cases or airport trolleys in their possession to avoid the inconvenience of tripping over her and/or her water bucket, however, she was transparent to most if not all who trampled past her.

Her employers did not value her enough to protect her hand from detergent or from the human bodily fluids that may have fallen to the floor from any of its three orifices, irrespective of age or condition; her whole being from infection; her back from injury; her knees or any part of her for that matter!

The thoughts, which immediately sprang into my head, were to first question what I had witnessed:

Was my reaction due to my heightened sensitivity to my new surroundings?

I may have been *just* looking for things?

I witness for myself how easily the letters 'd' and

'e' could be added to a perfectly good word such as 'humanization' to squeeze out all its respectability.

The explanation or justification, in the minds of the employer (usually costs) to oversee the dehumanization at such a basic level could not be easily understood.

What I saw had hit a nerve. A thought came to my mind.

For change to happen in South Africa it would take a whole lot of effort to shift from such mentally; because like the very act of breathing, it would take effort, consciousness and determination to suppress what came naturally.

Still in the airport our next stop was at the shop to buy a map of the local area. The cashier was a pale skinned girl who, with pimples which appeared as though its contents should have been expelled a long time ago, had her curly blond hair sat motionless on top of her head in the form of a 'bun'. Sharif paid for the few items with a Gold credit card he had owned for over ten years. The cashier took the card firmly from him with a quizzical look of scrutiny and disbelief (that he should own such a card) she examined the signature long and thoroughly prompting him to ask, "Is everything alright?"

On hearing his British accent, she grasped the card between thumb and forefinger extended her arm fully and with a swift flick of the wrist she invited him to take his card and simultaneously held his purchase extended towards him with her other hand.

The cashier spoke no words but her piercing blue eyes told volumes as they peered over the metal rim of her spectacles and followed us out of the shop; implying an Orwellian-type experience throughout the remainder of our stay. Even with the allowance for her role (as cashier in an airport) thus increasing the possibility of frequent encounters with fraudsters, which, she may have experienced; the girl's confidence and arrogance, for one appearing so young, was staggering and with deliberate and well-practiced gestures, suggesting that she was the one who was advanced in years (in a culture where a certain reverence is paid to elders), she was the one with power and authority and more crucial with this relatively brief but poignant encounter, she had the law on her side which she knew only too well.

Walking through the airport we discussed our encounters and decided that these were not holiday breakers but still an indication of what we could expect. It was also the moment that something changed in me.

I knew that my attitude and western mentality had to change radically to survive our new surroundings of South Africa!

Johannesburg

Thursday, 30 December

The tinted automatic doors opened to the blaze and brightness of the African sun forcing me to shield my eyes and find my shades quickly. Fumbling through my bag I came across my sunglasses I placed them on and had a fleetingly thought of the rain, darkness and 2 degrees Celsius we left behind in England.

A genteel, smooth-faced and honest-looking young Asian man approached us, informing us of his,

'Very comfortable coach service.'

That would take us directly to our hotel at a cost of,

'Only 40 Rand each.'

Which we calculate would work out to approximately £8 for each of us.

He also assured us that there was no 'ordinary' bus service from the airport to where we wanted to go and that taxis would be very costly. He kindly loaded our bags into the back of his clean van and seated us comfortably inside. He immediately returned inside the airport to try to enlist other new arrivals.

Situations when I would gladly surrender and pay-up whatever the cost, did not really apply to us, here, at this moment.

Such times that they might apply being: when travelling with young children, for safety reasons, for peace of mind, when completely exhausted (we were tired, but an excited tiredness), when trying desperately to impress someone (be it business or love) or when money is simply not a consideration. I am sure that there are other reasons; suffice to say well none applied.

Our wait inside the van was uncomfortable and we turned to our guidebook that had told us to avoid such services and to get an 'ordinary' bus.

We chose to follow the guidebook; so we collected our luggage travelled by bus to the main station (at a total cost of 15 Rand/£2.66) before getting a taxi (3 Rand/£0.53) to our hotel.

Taxis were dutifully lined up and were easy to access. When we had decided to travel to South Africa, a close friend of Sharif could not have spoken more highly of the Park Lane Hotel and its surrounding area of Hillbrow in Joburg.

'Aaah South Africa!' he had said with a broad South African laughter; which, I felt, was both sad and happy at the same time. 'Sad' because it was the country of his birth, which he had been in exile from for the past twenty years and 'happy' because if he could not be there then a good friend going was the next best thing.

Indeed we felt that he would have taken offence had we not booked our room and stopped to look elsewhere; after all did he not still know his own country and where the best places were?

So we stopped looking and secured our room at

the Park Lane Hotel, Hillbrow, Johannesburg, South Africa!

That is how we ended up staying at the Park Lane Hotel in Hillbrow.

Now that we had arrived the only issue with our friend's advice, was that, it was based on his knowledge of his beloved country over twenty years before.

We climbed into the taxi; the driver was upbeat and chatty as we settled on its back seat and were delivered speedily to our final destination of Hillbrow.

The car pulled to a halt outside the Park Lane Hotel and we stumbled out along with our luggage and into the foyer of the hotel. We took the taxi driver's number just in case we needed him again and he was happy to give it to us for the prospect of additional work.

Tired and hungry we struggled to complete the formalities of checking into the hotel. We were finally shown to our room by a slim, very smartly dressed gentleman of advanced years.

He held his head high and proud and walked very upright as though marching; the sort of person who when standing face to face your whole body responds by behaving as though it is being pulled up by the top of your head in a quest to appear as tall and as upright as he appeared.

We took advantage of his slight hesitation to continue with leaving our room; he hovered in the doorway as though trying to remember everything that he was supposed to do or say before leaving.

Wishing to question him about the hotel's history, life in South Africa, the surrounding area and where to go to celebrate the New Year; Sharif opened the conversation with:

'This is our first time in South Africa.'

He retreated backwards turning as he freed his hand from the door handle and re-entering the room fully.

'Oh, Sir, is that so?' with emphasis and curiosity his voice on the 'so'.

'Yes, with only one day to go before the celebrations really start, where is the best place to see the New Year in?'

What we did not expect was the advice that followed: he seemed to come to life and with added animation as he enacted his advice to us, which, conveyed emphasis and passion.

His advice to us, categorically, was to:

"Stay in your room and turn on the TV."

(He approached the TV and mimicked turning on the TV.)

"Sit back."

(He sat down in the armchair.)

"And watch TV (he leaned forward) on New Year's Eve and see the New Year in."

(He relaxed back in the armchair with a contented smile on his face.)

"On account of the previous year's violence and mayhem this was the best advice the hotel could give to you and your wife Sir."

He concluded and fell silent. As though to press the point he then ushered us over to one of the windows and as we looked down from on high (with him taking up the position in between us) he pointed to an innocuous creamy grey square building identifying it as one of the infamous 'hostels'.

'These places are no good. They are filled with migrant workers who are mostly young men and often erupting into violence.'

'Look,' he said, pointing to a few streets away from the hotel. 'The body of a man was found in the streets, right there.'

'Oh dear,' said I, looking nervous and concerned.

'Don't worry; you just have to be careful when you are out Madam. This hotel in its, heyday,' he continued proudly, 'hosted the ANC (African National Congress) officials,' he continued: 'this is where the ANC would hold their meetings.'

That last proud statement I seem to recall when it was being recommended to us, however, those 'glory days' happened a long time ago and things had obviously changed in Hillbrow Johannesburg.

We thanked him for everything and for making us feel so welcomed, tipped him and bid our good evenings.

We unpacked what we needed, freshened up and decided to sleep for one hour but it turned into three. On waking we showered and changed. We decided to eat in the hotel.

It was still five in the afternoon and the air was

moist and cool.

We decided to go for an early evening stroll.

Little did I know that I would witness something that would turn my thinking around yet again!

A Chance Encounter in Joburg

To describe Johannesburg is best done by its skyline – tower blocks and more tower blocks. The hustle and bustle of street life in all forms flourished in front of our eyes.

Street sellers with their wares neatly displayed in either plastic bags or on colourful polystyrene plates: three to four green apples, three mangoes, onions, tomatoes, potatoes and more.

The spicy aroma filled the air while young boys, for a small fee, occupied 'their patch' to look after cars where its owners had already parked alongside meters.

The solid women marched along with their babies tied close and cosily, in the same cloth as their outfits, to their backs; appear to be hurrying or were they just walking with purpose to prevent becoming targets? Who knows? But the scene taken in its entirety and seen for the first time by an 'outsider' seems to buzz with excitement!

Walking down the main street trying to take in all the new scenery; there, right there in front of the pharmacy I saw a tall white-haired man. He was a white man with a sign, which read:

PLEASE HELP SICK WIFE

And in his hand was a can (in which passers-by were invited to deposit their financial offerings).

This cannot be real, I thought... A white person

begging in South Africa!?

Further down the street another surprising sight.

In fact it was a more distressing sight that greeted us; that of an old woman in a shop doorway.

The parade of shops were closed and the white-haired woman supported by a Zimmer frame was leaning forward with her palm open and upturned so as to capture every Rand that came her way by any sympathetic passer-by.

Her once cream bandage around her calf was now a dirty grey and hanging from her affected limb exposing a sore. The woman's pink face appearing red and blotchy, from the now receded sun, appeared tired and drawn. Begging! This was unheard of in my little world that polarized the races.

This poor old white woman was left to beg on the streets at the mercy of whoever would take pity on her. To me this was shocking absolutely shocking to see this in South Africa.

Would I have been surprised if I had seen this in London? Yes, maybe I would but not as surprised as I was seeing it here. I thought that I had it worked out in my mind that the rich people were white and the poor people were black and although that still holds true for the most part the situation was not as clear cut and was rapidly unravelling.

We continued up the high street where there were several restaurants and settling for one with outside space we sat to watch the world go by and refreshed our thirst before returning to our hotel for the night.

Buses, Trains and Holidays!

We headed to the bus station with the intention to buy tickets out of Joburg; a ticket to somewhere or anywhere as long as it was out of Joburg. We ran forward and into the station only to be told, by a man dressed in uniform, that due to the holidays the buses were already closing down and reopening again on Monday. It may have been the desperate look on our faces why he volunteered the information that we could 'try the railway station' and directed us there.

We did try our luck at the railway station but it too was against us. The somewhere or anywhere north of South Africa was fully booked or closed for the holidays, with, the earliest movement at the train station being the 4 or 5 January, which was even later than the buses.

We returned to the bus station and purchased our tickets to Zimbabwe for Monday, 3 January.

With no way out of Johannesburg we conceded defeat due to poor planning and acknowledged that we were stuck here! Come-what-may we had to make the best of Hillbrow and Joburg until Monday, 3 January.

We left the station and headed to the ANC's offices with the intentions of buying a few books.

Once outside, the small office with its small glass panelled windows and green and yellow paint; was a far cry from what I had expected. I marvelled at how such humble beginnings could grow into such a world power force for political change. I thought how Mr Nelson Mandela must have touched the door handle and walked through this same doorway that I was about to walk through.

For me it was like entering into a religious shrine.

Inside there was a wooden desk to the left of the door and to the right a small table had lots of flyers and written articles; that were free to take (even though they needed every Rand in donations). We spoke in whispered voices (not that anyone told us to do so) there bookshelves were stacked with books for sale and it was from here where I chose to buy a book about 'the Struggle'.

We spoke briefly to the women who were there and also took away some literature before we left and made our way back to the hotel.

In the hotel we mulled over the advice that was given freely to us on our arrival, by the kind gentleman and decided to settle on having our dinner at the hotel restaurant.

The a-la-carte menu offered up a plentiful selection to choose from, of roast beef, mutton or fish; rice or roast potatoes and broccoli; the dessert choices were gateaux, fresh pineapple, or ice cream were all beautifully presented. Needless to say, that, we ate well.

After eating and enjoying the delicious meal we started talking to the head waiter about where we could go to celebrate New Year; to which he replied without hesitation and with emphasis:

'Johannesburg is even more dangerous than the

American New York.'

This reminded me of the advice that was given to us by the taxi driver, who, turned around and looking at us said:

'Please my brother and sister do me a favour?' At the time I thought, what could it be, since he hardly knew us?

'Travel light! No chains-no bags – just the minimum!' came his advice.

We enjoyed our meal and spent the evening in 'The Pub with no Name' where we met an Australian. Once we had revealed our plans to travel to Zimbabwe to him, he immediately assured us that he knew 'some very nice Zimbabweans'.

The hotel band that played was very good but by 02:30 we were exhausted and ready for bed.

Happy New Year!!

31 December – Saturday, 1 January 1994

This was New Year's Eve!

The year that would see a brand new dawn on South Africa!

'We really need to do something special Sharif?' I said. 'We need to remember where we were in the year of the free elections in South Africa.' He did not need any more convincing.

He ordered a taxi from our hotel room. It arrived and drove us to a recommended nightspot in the area of Newtown called Kippies named after Kippie Moeketsi the legendary jazz saxophonist (whose statue now stands outside the club).

That night of Friday, 31 December 1993 we danced the night away to Latin, Afro, and Caribbean Jazz and witnessed black people dancing with white people and vice versa; I witnessed that the people appeared to have a shared and healthy respect for each other and everybody was enjoying the beautiful mellow jazz music together!

Talented musicians took to the stage to rapturous applause and played as though they were never going to stop! The crowd loved every minute and asked for more! More! More!

We danced and danced.

We were so absorbed with what was happening inside the club that it completely slipped my mind of how we were going to get back to our hotel. Back in the UK, ordinarily it could be difficult getting a taxi on a Saturday and any major holiday would definitely need pre-booking a good while in advance. This thought, of returning to the hotel, was far, far away and at this moment would not have mattered anyway!

South Africa was on the verge of change! And anything was possible! We twisted and twirled our bodies in time to the beat with people that we had never met and would most probably never see again – but it did not matter and that became the reason for dancing some more!

After being cocooned in the cosy, energetic, hot, smoky atmosphere of the club and meeting new 'friends' we emerged, in the early hours, to the warm night air under the clear African skies; our feet aching but having had a wonderful time. With the reality of our situation only now dawning on us, we began to look around for a way to get back to our hotel. Not having any success to secure a taxi on our own, we returned inside the club to seek out our new 'friends' who we hoped would be able to help us.

After several attempts they were able to order a taxi for us and told us of the difficulties that they had. We thanked them and told them that we were very grateful but neither of us could understand why the taxis were refusing to come to this beautiful part of the town.

The taxi eventually turned up and we snuggled in, thinking ourselves as being very lucky and with our comfortable hotel-beds beckoning all was well. I relaxed back in the seat for the driver to do his thing and drive us back to the hotel; but he wanted to talk. How inconsiderate, I thought, since having exited the club, the music still ringing in my ears and the cool night air... sleep began to descend, I was struggling to keep my eyes open; like arm wrestling back and forward movement but now it was up and down with my eye lids. I was losing the fight with my own eye lids.

What is the matter with this man? I thought. He appeared agitated, nervous and eager to get out of the vicinity; he was watchful as he held the car steering wheel tightly and close to his chest with his chin peering over the top of the rim and his eyes on high alert watchfulness.

About a couple miles from the start of our journey, all became clear; there was an eerie stillness with hardly anyone on the streets. What surrounded us were only the remnants of what had gone before.

We were being transported through what resembled a war zone!

Walls were torn down, cars were burnt out or turned over, tall trees were pushed over or somehow uprooted and the streets were littered with debris of all manner, shapes and sizes.

It was the skill of the driver who avoided unexpected obstacles in the road, that enabled the car to swerve left then right, drive fast then faster, sway right, turn and turn again, then slow and slower; then eventually normal driving until we reached our destination.

On arriving back at the hotel, safely and to the relief of all of us, we tipped heavily asked if he would be all right? He assured us that his way home would **not** take him in the same direction from which we had just come, so he would be okay.

We bid our expert driver farewell and wished him a 'Happy New Year!'

Saturday Afternoon, 1 January 1994

Gold Reef City

We woke late: in fact it was closer to midday.

'That's what holidays are for,' I hear my mum saying!

So no guilt and in trying to decide what we would do and today being a holiday meant that most places would be closed to business; our options were limited.

Johannesburg has been built on its gold.

With its history, in relation to gold mining, resulting in some catastrophic accidents for the miners, who may only have wanted the opportunity to have a steady job that would provide for themselves and their families rather than a job that they would have to pay for the privilege of doing with their lives.

Democracy is driven by the free market and therefore making the maximum in profits is the ultimate aim. Mining is no different. Those who are willing to cut corners on safety to maximize profits may be few but the outcome can be devastating when things go wrong.

The many 'someone else's son' (father, brother, grandfather) killed in the South African mines have been numerous and there is no shortage of young men vying for the position of 'miner' and who are instantly replaceable by 100 others waiting to take that coveted place.

When major accidents in South African mines have been reported on our TV in the UK, the general attitude is one of: – clean up and lets press on – but I wondered if or how these men have been remembered? Are there any memorial plaques or their names carved in stone anywhere?

The hostels are where migrant workers such as miners would live whilst away from their families. These hostels were cited as being major causes of AIDS (acquired immune deficiency syndrome) spreading rampantly in South Africa.

We were intrigued to find out more about this glossy place called Gold Reef City.

We wanted to see for ourselves how the gold was mined but not knowing anyone with such connections or where were the best places to go; and these feelings being compounded by knowing that we would not be allowed anywhere, even, close to a real mine; we had to find another place to visit.

We set off to find the Gold Reef City to see how the gold that built Johannesburg was mined.

One of the guides in the Gold Reef City was a round-face, muscular and well-built chap; he stood proudly by the furnace, as though he himself had built and owned it outright.

However, searching a little deeper, I was acutely aware of his display of pride. Pride that he was trusted to handle the gold bars; yes that was his pride. He had a very responsible job of taking out and positioning these bars in the mornings, talking about them and locking them away at night. It was he that the boss trusted to do this job and no other.

He stood beside the heavy long metal 'plank' with a conveyor mechanism; designed to roll the hot gold bars out for shaping. This metal 'plank' jutted out into the middle of the room and back into a crescent shaped open brick oven, which was blazing red/yellow/white heat.

The visitors stood away but close enough to hear him speak.

He was eloquent with telling the history of the gold rush and the founding fathers and so forth. He talked about the Boer wars and the sacrifices made during this time.

It is intriguing how the conquer has an incessant need to tell his story and in so doing rewrites history.

Finally he talked about the process of making the gold bars and offering up a challenge to the crowd: 'Whoever can pick up the solid gold bar with two fingers was allowed to keep it.'

It remained in his possession till this day, of this, I am certain.

Sunday, 2 January

Sun City

Today was another day of nothing to do.

Sun City, we heard, was an obscene display of wealth gone completely mad. This is where the 'stars' came to perform when they, 'went to South Africa'.

In my mind's eye I saw a huge indoor space, similar to the portrayal on our TV screens back in the UK of Las Vegas; with machines for gambling eateries and bars; I also imagined other air conditioned rooms with high ceilings elaborately decorated in gold, cream with marbled floors; flamboyant statues would be placed strategically throughout the venue to represent opulence and grandeur (as far away as possible from the reality of the outside world). Then my imagination took me to the space where the performances would take place: singers, cabaret artists, dancers and a complete spectrum of entertainers would risk reputation and having their life changed forever to perform in the 'Grand Hall'.

Here, I imagined everything as before only bigger and more opulent. There were Roman columns, indoor water fountains, palm trees, exotic flowers purposely flown into South Africa from any country around the world. Marble not only on the floors but walls too, and chandeliers as big as I could imagine glistened and shone its bright yet warm glow on each and every visitor to absolve any guilt or hesitation that they ought not be here. The enticing light told each visitor that this is what they deserved, this is what real life is about… enjoy and come back again soon.

We took a bus and set out to see Sun City.

The entrance of Sun City had huge displays of carved animals, giving the impression (may be rightly) that they were carved directly out of the red rock that is common to the area. The Lion and Elephant which towered over the entrance were carved in a position of relaxation, which, suggested that I too could relax.

The Elephant stood upright with trunk hanging downwards and head in a comfortable neutral position; the Lion rested on its stomach, with its head held tall and proud, and only one of its paws casually draped downwards could be seen (the others which I imagined were curled cosily under him) representing a state of 'just fed' contentment. The carvings as a whole gave the appearance of alertness, feelings of protection and a reminder, to those who needed reminding, that they were in Africa.

Surrounded by dense forestry Sun City was like an oasis; a place where Mother Nature had chosen vegetation over sand and sea but mankind like a spoilt child would stop at nothing to get what it wanted; and so created its own sand and sea.

The central creamy white building opened out on both sides, like the wings of a great bird, with other buildings attached to it both left and right and then more attached again. The whole site screamed 'look at me!' without any attempt made to blend in with its surroundings.

On the tall walls that surrounded the complex, were, what looked like plastic moulds of animals, positioned to appear like authentic carvings; a funfair with children's rides was visible in the distance. At the rear of the buildings were parasol-covered restaurants and a large replica beach, which, I imagined was reserved for guess that were staying at the hotels.

We followed the wide grey stone-slab path as we made our way to a wooden-frame, wall-free and roughly thatched hut; which had the smoothest red-earth floor that any professional plasterer would be proud to claim ownership; there stood a heavily tanned young man in a straw hat announcing the next show:

'At 1:45; the next show will be "The Gun Boot Dance" which will be in only six minutes.' Using the time before the performance the young man continued:

'The Gun Boot Dance originated with miners who sang and danced while hitting their boots to keep timing and added rhythm (in the absence of any instruments).'

As he spoke, my mind drifted.

Just like Sea World or any such places (for that matter) where several times during the day there is a 'performance of a type'; Sun City was no different, only, this time the performers were not seals, dolphins or penguins; they were black men; who were brought out to perform in front of a crowd. So at the appointed time, emerging from behind the straw-weaved screen at the back of the smooth-dirt-floor hut, the men walked out in an orderly fashion; one behind the other and stood in the middle of the hut facing the crowd.

The five men, with the exception of their helmets, were all dressed the same: heavy dark blue cotton dungarees, which were worn shirtless, tucked into thick black rubber boots and on their heads were plastic helmets in colours of white, blue, yellow, red and green.

The five men lined up and with a swift count of 1...2...3...They burst into song with a level of energy (I have rarely seen in this heat) they began to dance. In unison they lifted their boot-clad feet inwards at the knees and slapped their thick black boots on either side using one hand then the other in quick succession. This same dance movement was reversed on the other leg separated by only a small jump for them to change leg.

Everything happened very quickly and the boot-slapping movement formed the basic chorus between verses likened to any popular hymn sang in church on a happy Sunday morning in the UK.

Here the dance verses included: a small leap in the air, a full circular turn and even a short quick step backward then forwards, in displays of perfect timing, rhythms and with exacting pauses they moved as one and held the crowd's attention.

Now the second part of the show began allowing each man to have a turn in the limelight to perform some act of individuality. The other four men, with their hands clasped firmly behind their backs, stood in line behind the individual performer. This allowed the line of men to be used as the length of a small imaginary stage.

Starting from left to right the first performer stepped forward; he leapt in the air; jumping with both legs outstretched in front of him and arching forward he touched the end of his upturned toes. He landed firmly on the ground with only the disturbance of dust rising from beneath his boots to betray his sudden and explosive movements. The height he managed to reach was amazing and displayed his high level of fitness. This movement was repeated the length of the 'stage' and back again before he fell back into line and was immediately replaced by the second performer.

The performer ran forward and sat on the ground with legs outstretched. In an instant he hoisted himself up off the ground with his muscular arms and began to twist and turn the lower half of his body (a scene more familiar in a gymnasium competition performed on the back of a wooden horse); he circled his body round and round raising his hands at the perfect time to allow the rest of his body to pass.

The third performer lifted each leg in turn high in the air, assuming the position of an exaggerated march and clapping between each stride; he marched and clapped up and down the line of men before resuming his position in the line.

The fourth man assumed a Russian dance, by bending down then jumping back into a standing position immediately. When in the upright position with both his legs extended and opened wide, he balanced on the back heal of his boots before bending down again. Once again with energy he went forward then backwards along the 'stage'.

When compared with what had gone before I

thought that the last man came forward looking timid and almost apologetic. He simply balanced on one hand with his feet together and extended in the air, forming the perfect image of a human arrow; for what seemed like the longest time, before flicking his whole body back into a standing position.

I loved it and gave him the loudest cheer and the crowd did too by the rousing applause. All the time the tanned young man looked on.

The atmosphere was cooled right down by the singing of a 'traditional' song, which, I took to mark the ending of the performance.

They sang a 'clicking song' a language of mainly the Xhosa and Zulu people and made worldwide popular by Miriam Makeba's song 'Qongqothwane' or the clicking song.

The deep baritones and rousing sentiments (going by the facial expressions) accompanied by the banging of the chest and now a more restrained and determined dance movements showed a proud and passionate people.

The crowd clapped again and asked for 'more!' and threw coins to show their thanks for an end to an excellent, worthy and energetic performance.

We appreciated the Gun Boot Dance but not even that could have kept us in Sun City any longer and so we made our way to our hotel.

Monday, 3 January

Expats Unite

The next day we headed to the heart of Joburg and so to East Gate Shopping Centre. We both stood trying to figure out where we were on the map and in so doing figure out the direction we needed to go. It happened very quickly that one-minute there were just the two of us then the next second a red faced white man was looking at the map too and saying in a jolly friendly manner:

'Are you lost, here let me help you?'

Before we could reply he took charge of the map and ushering us to the side near some shops he continued, 'This place can be a bit of a bugger, I heard your accents and figured out that you were fellow Brits, are you here long?'

Sharif and I looked at each other. We also were able to have a good look at our rescuer! He was dressed smart but casual in brown shorts and a light blue short-sleeved cotton shirt and a hat like those worn by umpires at cricket matches. He was a rather tall man with a rather a large and bulbous nose.

He told us that he was from England but made this his home over thirty years ago. He had made lots of money but lost it all through his love of drink and becoming an addict; he now devotes his time to Alcoholics Anonymous from which he was travelling to go home.

He dipped into his pocket of his shirt and pulled out a business card, handing it to Sharif he said, 'This is me and the offices where I work.'

Ken told us that he lived in Stanton, which was quite an affluent suburb. Durban was where many Asians and Coloureds lived.

Turning his upper body in his direction of intended travel he said unexpectedly: 'Why don't you come with me, come and see how ordinary South Africans live?'

Well it was like we were caught up in a whirlwind and we now had to make a decision. We chatted briefly at a short distance away from him and decided that because we were more in number and that he seemed harmless enough that we would follow him.

Ken's home was a modest gated bungalow. He asked us to wait outside while he put his dogs out the back and as promised he appeared again inside and beckoned us to join him. Quite a shabby bachelor pad, he busied himself with making tea while explaining that all the homes had gates/dogs or both, with some having electric fences.

Ken told us that despite the fact that South Africa had been good to him, he fully realised that the inequality could not continue. He told us that the shutters/gates and or dogs were a sign of how people were living in fear of violence and therefore there was a price that is being paid daily for ill-gotten gains. He said that what happens after April was everyone's concern. We chatted for a while longer.

We thanked him and he pointed us on our way.

SECTION 3

JANUARY 3-15, ZIMBABWE

Five Hours and Still Counting

Monday, 3 January

The earliest journey out of Johannesburg was Monday, 3 January by bus since the trains did not start running for another couple days after this. We hesitated for a slight moment and then Sharif purchased the ticket to Zimbabwe. We agreed to travel at night so we could arrive in the daylight and have sufficient time to find a hotel.

On the day of our travel, we packed a few provisions we had bought at the supermarket earlier and headed for the bus at the Rotunda Travel Centre. Amongst the hustle and bustle of those who appeared to know exactly where they were negotiating their way to and from; we managed to find our Grey Hound bus in the station waiting and ready for our 22:30 departure time.

We duly settled down in seats towards the front of the bus in our seats and thought of what would lie ahead of us on a bus journey that would take seventeen hours to complete.

The driver checked all the tickets and made himself

as comfortable as he could before starting the engine and then began to roll the bus out of the station.

Feeling relieved that we were finally on our way we eased our self into our seats, hoping that it would hug us and let us know that all would be alright. Most of the passengers on the almost full bus, at some point fell asleep, huddled under coats; those fortunate enough to have packed in a more prepared, and experienced manner, had a blanket and travel pillow which frankly made little or no difference to the comfort ratings of trying to sleep on a bus.

We hurtled through the pitch blackness of the night.

The first couple hours into the journey I tried to stay awake for not wanting to miss anything but soon succumbed to the darkness of the night.

Before falling asleep I had desperately tried to stay awake being petrified of the following:

One, the driver not being able to stay awake throughout the night (causing us to crash); two, animals running into the path of the oncoming bus (causing us to crash); and three the thought of the bus breaking down.

I had to be the driver's 'other pair of eyes'; not that I was asked, or should any or all three of the above have happened I would be the one cowering in the back but still… I needed to stay awake.

I had focused my eyes on the front of the bus and its headlights, which, did not extend beyond its immediate path ahead. I focused then focused some more until I was hypnotized by the headlights and the soothing hum of the engine and fell into a deep but uncomfortable sleep.

I awoke at dawn to the view of a narrow but surprisingly flat dirt road which like a ball of wool just kept unravelling. The faster the bus travelled the more roads there were ahead of it. The meagre road was unforgiving where water from too much rain had caused damage to the red earth and tossed the bus up and down over pot-holes jolting us out of our seat or at times our sleep. The road went on for miles and miles as far as the eye could see.

The thought came to me that we had another ten hours on a bus duty bound for Zimbabwe along this dusty red dirt road; interspersed only by small villages and wooden shacks sparsely stocked of provisions representing the only shop for miles.

The geographical positioning of Zimbabwe away from the sea ports means that fresh provisions have to travel an arduous route to reach its destination. It also struck me that these land-locked countries were dependent on others who had seaports and therefore could be politically vulnerable.

The round thatched houses, so made to encourage coolness by the efficient circulation of air, flashes by as the bus bounded through village after village. Same welcome time after time of children smiling with excitement at the approach of the bus and simultaneously waiting for the danger to pass before chasing after it; running, running as fast as their little feet could take them only stopping when exhausted and the realisation dawning that the twenty wheeled monster is faster than they could ever be. In a display of good sportsmanship their small arms outstretched and resting on their bent knees, they acknowledge the loss to a faster opponent, raise their eyes to smile once more and wave to the bus as it leaves their village for the next in a hail of dry African dust and heat.

The driver cooled himself by having his small window wide and as open as his faded yellow cotton shirt, which, when full of air then flapped about all around him beating lightly on his exposed flesh.

'Pass me the water,' he requested of his mate, who I assumed was to be the second river and whom I had not noticed before, duly fulfilled the request and passed the bottle of water to him.

The exchange between them was so seamless yet so simple. It conveyed a friendship and understanding of partners who had been around each other for a long time.

With the bottle in hand he held it above his head allowing its contents to fall out on him running down from the top of his head to his chest and beyond. His colleague meanwhile without any prompt took the bottle from him allowing him to use his right hand to rub his face while steadying the bus with his left hand.

'That feels good,' said the first driver, now almost completely dry again from the heat.

They talked and laughed and caught up on news until the second driver, in preparation for his turn at the wheel, fell into a deep sleep that delivered a snore so loud that, had the bus stood still, could have caused a herd of elephants to stampede. Even though a few people were trying to rest also no one on the bus uttered a word of complaint, the reasoning being that the more rested he was the safer we all would be when it was his turn to drive and so he was left to rest without disturbance.

Three or four times during the journey not counting the official stops (where all the passengers got off the bus) one or either of the drivers would stop the bus and run out of view to relieve himself of the water he had drank earlier, returning to the bus he would announce:

'We will now continue;' before taking up his position at the wheel of the bus once more.

Several hours later in the heat of the early afternoon, it felt like a treat, from a parent to a child, when approaching a village the driver announced:

'Don't get off the bus but I will allow a few of the village women to come to you for a short time to show you what they have for you.'

The bus came to a halt underneath a tall tree with a wide girth, on the side of the road, which opened out its leaves and branches like the type of big umbrella commonly paraded by sports men and women. The bus creaked and cracked as it attempted to cool under the sparse shade that the tree could give to such a large customer.

There were three women each balancing on their heads different anticipated delights as they slowly walked gracefully and in a line towards the bus.

The first woman held onto the handle bars and heaved one hip then rocking her body, skilfully, to the other side dragged her other leg up and onto the steps of the bus.

Followed by the other two women in quick succession.

Here the first woman stood at the front of the bus tall and elegant; dressed in a long pink cotton skirt which was heavily embroidered and from the knees the skirt 'fanned out' as if it were a fish's tail and hinted at curvatures beneath. In contrast, on her upper-half, she wore a plain cotton scooped-neck short sleeved top in a lighter pink that complimented her dark complexion and suited her round 'pleasant' looking face. She smiled and introduced herself as Elizabeth.

Mary was much shorter than Elizabeth, reaching just beneath her chin. Slim and agile and seeming as though she had boundless energy. Her eyes were gentle and strict at the same time. Gentle to potential customers but gave off a sense of firmness (maybe because this was business and she was in her office). Her knee-length light blue cotton dress was more western in its plain fabric and 50s style.

And last came Ruth; a round, heavier woman than the first two and with a much more engaging character that I warmed to immediately. Ruth appeared 'fun' making you feel as though she was putting herself out in order to please you; in fact a 'true' business woman.

Immediately and expertly one by one they dismounted their wares from their heads and formed a line to walk down the aisle of the bus thus allowing each seat of two passengers, the space and time to view without interruption (from the other two) and to contemplate their decision of whether or not to part with their money in semi privacy. It was like peering in through the seller's own shop window as they filed passed.

First seller Elizabeth: had small-boxed drinks, edible home made provisions such as roasted corn on the cob and small lighters.

Second seller Mary: had the most beautiful crochet tops for children and a few squares of traditionally dyed clothes, tins and cleaning clothes.

Third seller Ruth: had small items carved out of local wood such as animals, birds and all manner of things that suddenly I could envisage a purpose that may have eluded its creator and I did not know that I needed.

The passengers, though already tired of the journey and the heat, were pleased for the brief respite of the humming of the tyres against the dry road and so purchased anything that could be used to ease the journey or give as small gifts. The boxed drinks were very popular prompting Elizabeth to give a broad smile causing her almond shaped eyes to light up as she rushed excitedly off the bus to refill her stock. Ruth also did well with her small wooden carvings; I could not resist buying a small elephant from her and of course because of Ruth's engaging manner other passengers purchased items too.

The women made their way off the bus having thanked and waved goodbye to us, presumably to await the next bus that will pass through their village.

Signals that the end of the journey was in sight came after I fell asleep again and another waking up to what was a less rural environment than what I had now become used to seeing out of the windows of the bus. My heart skipped a beat at the anticipation of our imminent arrival in Harare.

I sat up to look out and take in everything as far as I could see as the bus rolled into town: traffic lights, street markets, high rise buildings, people and more people rushing, the noise of a town on the move, the dust (some would say dirt) filled the air. Gone were the green trees, smiling faces, slow pace of life, children running after the bus and the sound of birds singing.

We arrived in Zimbabwe just before four in the afternoon to the buzz of a metropolis.

And so our journey came to an end as the bus turned into the bus depot. The passengers reached for their small cases some of which were stored overhead and in an orderly fashion set down off the bus.

The drivers jumped off the bus to open up its under carriage and by using a long thick stick with a hook at the end, they were able to retrieve the larger suitcases from the well of the bus.

The grateful passengers, like us, thanked the drivers with a tip and clutching our now identified luggage we became part of the nebulous Harare crowd.

Harare

We entered the centre of Harare and booked in at the International Quality Inn Hotel on Baker Avenue and thought it wise to sleep for at least a couple hours before we set about discovering what Zimbabwe's capital city had to offer.

Harare appeared clean and orderly and we noticed the presence of police on (what seemed like every) street corners. We felt safer than we did in Johannesburg. Now being apart of the city and it being in the early evening Harare felt calmer than South Africa; prompting us to take a walk around the town in the evening. We cautiously approached every new road and being very relieved that not a single problem was ever encountered. We returned to the hotel.

Realising that a good source for local information was the workers in the hotel, in the evening, we struck up a conversation with the waiter. Who told us that President Mugabe was not a very popular President because the people were suffering and although they wanted to support him and are trying to 'hold out' times were very hard. He spoke of the disappointment of ten years of Mr Mugabe being the President because most of the ordinary people could not see any changes in their daily lives.

He spoke of the 'street boys' being a problem and how some restaurants encourage them by giving them food at the end of the day.

The following day as we emerged out of the hotel; we felt a bright hot and drier heat. A heat much more intense than we had experienced in South Africa; I quickly purchased a straw hat with remnants of straw falling all around the hat which enabled me, with a turn of the head, to brush away any small flying insects from in front of the face without lifting a hand to do so. I am convinced that I looked a 'spectacle' and not a good one; but quite frankly did not care since my newly purchased contraption satisfied keeping the sun away from me and eased the strain of me having to constantly brush things away from my face.

In this heat I moved only when I had to.

We settled for lunch at what looked like a popular spot and whilst eating worked out how much money we needed to exchange at the bank to allow us to pay for our planned four nights and three days canoeing experience down the Zambezi River in Mana Pool National Park.

We entered the bank and saw a never before sight in the UK, that of an all-black counter staff in the bank. Back in the UK we would consider it fortunate if we saw one black person in a bank.

People were in positions of power and authority and so displayed a confidence we had never witnessed before. It was truly wonderful to see and experience; as this followed through in restaurants, shops, hotels and just about everywhere that we went.

Unlike South Africa; in Harare people of colour were visible once more. They smiled and looked me in the eyes; there were no visible tell-tale sign of the mouth saying one thing and the eyes saying another. There were no visible (to the onlooker) signs, on faces or in posture, of shame, disappointment or hopelessness. No suggestion or questioning if s/he could *really* do the job. No playing to a 'Master Overseer' who threatened yours and your children's very existence day in day out.

There was none of that here just the opposite of: confidence, happiness, relaxed atmosphere, aspiration, dreams yet to be made real and a pride in just being.

It dawned on me that this must be how some people in the UK feel all the time. They just sail through the world unhindered, without this added stress that people of colour have as an appendage but only when it is removed is the realization of the heaviness of the weight that has been a constant companion.

We decided to exchange £300 into z\$ (Zimbabwean dollars).

The cashier counted out what we had previously calculated as being the correct exchange that we would receive and was prepared to step away from the counter; she, however, reached under her counter position and grabbed another handful of notes and began to count it on top of the pile that was already there; this action was repeated another three times before she eventually gave us the piles of cash and smiling pushed the documentation underneath the glass partition.

A little perplexed we quickly emptied one of the ruck sacks and started stuffing the cash into it until the bag was crammed full Z$ and saying:

'Thank you,' as we left the bank.

The exchange rate had hit the floor between us leaving the UK and arriving in Zimbabwe; a bit of vital information that we were quite ignorant of; until we walked out of the bank feeling the richest that we had ever felt.

Suddenly finding ourselves in the open and on the street we felt very conscientious about the amount of money we had tucked into the ruck sack. Not wanting to appear any different having come out of the bank, than when we first entered and deliberately wanting to act 'normal' so as not to attract attention.

But sometime, just sometimes the more you try, the less you achieve.

Sharif started walking close, very close to me; both our hands were holding one ruck sack, we then both realized at the same time and let go, so it fell to the floor, both now bending to pick it up our heads collided.

To calm our nerves we agreed to enter a shoe shop to purchase a pair of much needed sandals for me. We would afterwards go to pay for the expedition and that would have disposed of much of the cash.

The sandals cost the equivalent of £4 for what would be over £20 in the UK. We purchased other bits and pieces including a note book (in which I began to document my extra ordinary holiday) before setting off to find a travel agent.

To explore further, in the early evening, we walked around Harare and took in our new surroundings.

Having seen groups of street kids roaming around in large gangs and having had them spoken about by our gentleman at the hotel; my natural reaction was to hold everything closer to me for fear of it being snatched away and lost forever.

Not surprisingly, most of the kids walked without shoes; not through choice but rather through necessity, that is, they needed to walk and they did not have shoes to put on their feet. They looked meagre with eager restless eyes seeking out opportunities for their next meal.

When a small gang of about five kids passed by hurriedly it was noticeable that one child, of about nine years old, hung back from the rest of his crowd by walking at a slower pace than the rest of them until he was a pace or two in front of us.

He stopped in front of me and turned to face me squarely, looked directly at me before rocking his little body-frame in quick small movements from left to right, then, without warning he took a big step forward placing his foot down on the ground with a stamp, as though, to startle me (which it did). Opening his mouth to reveal pearly white teeth he let out a laugh, which, came from his stomach (far older than his years). On hearing his laughter, the others looked back and laughed too before he turned his back to us, caught up with his crowd and they all quickened to a jogging pace and disappeared out of sight ahead of us.

6-9 January

Thursday, 6 January

Sharif spent a long time telephoning to eventually book a flight to Kariba and Victoria Falls returning to Harare for us to leave on Saturday, 8 January for a canoeing adventure beginning on Sunday. We felt settled now that we had a plan for the next stage of our holidays.

Friday, 7 January: Christopher

Today we took a local bus out of Harare to Epworth to see the Bulungi (or Balancing) Rocks.

Epworth is a small village closest to the Matopos National Park where the Rocks can be found. As we got off the bus, I headed for the local shop to get a cold drink. Having refreshed and standing to consider our direction of travel a boy, small in stature, came up and introduced himself to us and offered his hand for a handshake to seal the introductions.

This was Christopher, a young man of ten years old, from the village of Epworth who had finished school for the day and now was free to occupy himself until his mother or sister called him to eat dinner.

Our hearts warmed to Christopher immediately.

Christopher walked with us telling us that he wanted to work hard at school so that he could become a doctor; he also offered to show us around his village and to take us somewhere really special.

Christopher took us across grassland and watched our face as he showed us the first of the many balancing rocks.

'See! Isn't that wonderful Sir?' he said to Sharif.

Balancing Rocks appeared on Zimbabwe bank notes (L): nr. Epworth

'Come with me and I will show you many more, and I will take you to my favourite one,' and with excitement he scampered ahead of us leaving us to follow him.

We talked and talked and Christopher told us that if he had one wish it would be to have a 'bicycle of my very own'.

'Well do you think that if you had many more tourists and saved very hard you might be able to get a bicycle?' I asked.

'Ooh No Ma`am.'

'Why not?' I probed further.

'It is because there is only one bicycle in the whole village and it belongs to a very important man. I am not as important yet.'

And with that he smiled and with a bounce in his step he continued with gusto and enthusiasm to show us round and introduced all the rocks with names and all the information that he kept in his little head about them.

The rocks took their resting places in gravity-defying positions, some balancing on top of each other; the sheer size of some of the stones should mean that they ought to fall over but no; they stand independently proud and erect and await the next tourist to gasp in wonder.

Local people have given names to each and can be directed around the area by following the named rocks.

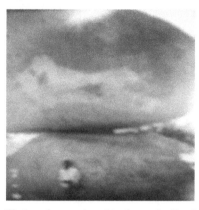

Christopher against his favourite Rock.

At the end of our guided tour we were escorted back to the bus stop and said our goodbyes. For one day only Christopher might have been the richest boy in the village as we emptied our pockets and purse of change. He beamed with a smile at his two small hands full of coins, he ran towards his home.

Saturday, 8 January: Just a Romantic Walk

Woken by the alarm call we caught a domestic flight to Kariba at 07:30 arriving forty-five minutes later.

A local taxi drove us from the small airport to the Cutty Sark Hotel where we had pre-booked our reservations.

The temperature was 34 plus and it was stifling, the heat was such that we had never known. On arriving we made our way directly to the outdoor bar in the grounds of the hotel.

The barman, eyed us up and down, not quite knowing what to make of us as we approached him for refreshments. We sat at the bar but were quickly shown tables and informed that our drinks would come to us. We duly obeyed, found a table and sat down and were rewarded almost immediately.

'Thank you, is it always this hot?' I said as he carefully laid the ice cold drinks on the tablemat.

'It has been known to reach in the 40s and we are expecting it later this week,' was the reply.

The owners were white Zimbabweans and they had a spectacular place. Positioned in beautiful scenery with the Kariba Dam in the distance and surrounded by lush vegetation (which given the temperature one would not ordinarily expect without an exceptional irrigation system).

To the front of the hotel and directly in the middle of its grounds, there stood an old tree; the trunk of the tree was so large that two adults with arms outstretched could not circle its circumference. Its branches extended outwards from the centre and hung down with dense leaves forming the shape of a very large parasol, which, may have been manually protection from the elements to all God's creatures (I could just as easily imagine an elephant or giraffe before the hotel was here); this was the function that the old tree adopted; for all who wanted to be sheltered from the weather be it rain or burning sunshine the tree would oblige.

In the night the tree provided much needed light from its many rainbow coloured bulbs expertly hung;

which lit up the hotel and the surrounding grounds.

On this first evening at the Cutty Sark Hotel and after dinner had been eaten and a drink had been drunk; Sharif thought it wise for us to continue our walk not only around the well-lit hotel but to venture out further, where the bright light did not throw itself.

'How will we see?' I asked.

'It is a full moon and we will be able to see by the moon,' he replied all dewy-eyed.

I can be rather sensitive to different environments, until that is, I adjust and am able to make sense of certain elements of my new surroundings. Here something did not feel right, so I replied:

'No I don't think so, maybe we could explore a bit more in the morning before we leave?'

He was not pleased but was fine with that. Instead we decided to take a taxi to a small village close by. The taxi driver without any prompting told us about wild animals such as cheetahs and lions who have been known to snatch people in the night. He was emphatic that under no circumstances must we go walking around these places at night.

A close escape I would say.

Sunday, 9 January

Up early we breakfasted and sat patiently in the reception area waiting to be collected for our canoeing adventure for the next three days and four nights down the Zambezi River. We waited and:

Waited some more.

We were expecting to be collected between 07:30 and 08:30 and it was now 9 a.m. where could they be? Had they forgotten us? We began to panic a little. Sharif rang the contact number that was given to us on booking. There was no reply. We sat and waited some more.

The crew arrived at 09:15.

We were OFF!
But not forgetting my hat!

My Hat.

9-12 January

Four Night and Three Days on the Zambezi River

We stopped periodically to collect the others: Jenny, Amily, Giles, Gwen, Berol, (Sharif, Shirley), Henora (the experienced Zimbabwean Leader/Guide) and Scott (Trainee Guide). Leon, the driver arrived at the check in reception at approximately 2:30. The journey through the Manna Pool National Park had taken just over four hours of driving through the park itself. Back in the UK it would take me one and half hours to drive from London to Birmingham; and here we were hardly any distance inside the Park after four hours.

Having showed our passport and immunization status forms we completed the formalities and entered the Manna Pool National Park; it took a total of seven hours to reach our destination of the starting point for our trip down the Zambezi River in a two man canoe for a once-in-a-life time expedition.

Our guides were one young white man in his late teens early twenties and the most experienced guide an older man called Henora.

Henora, I considered to be tall at a guess, just under six feet, his square jaw was a fitting frame for his broad and muscular shoulders, wide accommodating smile and with his deep-set eyes, all came together nicely. Henora had a quiet contemplative manner that gave the impressions that he was not only in charge but he was always thinking ahead of everyone else. Giving the impression of extensive experience and as though nothing could take him by surprise.

I felt secure with Henora at the helm.

Henora later explained to me and Sharif that the law was that only Zimbabweans could own companies, so, now the Settlers have had children who would be classed as Zimbabweans because they were born in Zimbabwe (unlike in Britain where to be called British there has to be proof of at least two generations).

The company that we had booked with made it their rule that each expedition had to have two people and one had to be the learner in order to be shown the 'ropes'. Henora said that he recognised that this was a gradual transition to the inexperienced 'now' native Zimbabwean and although it was annoying he was powerless.

Henora told the group that it would be best to set out about 4 p.m. with a view to setting up camp at around 6 p.m. since it was cooler by then and it would mean that we would not be too exhausted on our first venture out in the canoes.

There were a total of seven adventurers, one (turn taking too) share the canoe with the junior guide, making a total convoy of five canoes.

The Lead Guide, Henora had a two-man canoe with the space being filled with provisions for the journey.

We had an extensive safety talk and practised canoeing on land before placing them in the water and close to the bank for more practise. We packed our two man canoe and sat listening to stories which had the desired effect of making us petrified to set foot in the canoes. I truly wanted to leave and retrace my steps back to the hotel. But there were no taxis up here!

First Henora told us of the American man who insisted on disobeying the orders of not taking photos of the animals using a flash camera. The man then decided instead to video a Hippopotamus, even, standing up whilst his wife paddled. Unbeknown to him he was filming through the zoom lens, a fact he realized too late because the animal was upon him. With a bite to his leg he had to be air lifted to hospital while the animal had to be destroyed.

There was another story of a person being bitten by an unknown creature and had symptoms so severe that he had to be air lifted to hospital too. After he finished telling us these tales and without flinching he got up and continued to show us how to push our canoes off safely.

We were off!!

The vastness of the Zambezi was breathtaking. Travelling down it with Zambia on the left and Zimbabwe on the right we slithered in an orderly line behind our two guides. About an hour into our journey Henora, took us away from the bank and pointed back towards the land, where we could clearly see crocodiles sunning themselves in the heat. Crocodiles sun themselves in order to raise their body temperature, Henora told the group; when their body temperature is raised they are able to run faster; and beneath the rough shell-like covering crocodiles are solid muscle; well able to kill animals twice their size, such as adult Wildebeest, by creeping up on them (as they bend their heads to drink from the river).

We continued down until the guide signalled that we would stop and set up camp.

He pulled in to a small piece of sand and dragged our canoes one by one onto the strip. Here we were given four metal poles and mosquito netting along with an air mat and a sleeping bag. We chose our spot whilst the guides set about preparing a very tasty dinner. We sat around talking for a while and were advised to go to bed in preparation for our first full day ahead.

That's when it dawned on me; I had to sleep under the stars!!

That first night I imagined lions roaring in the yonder, hippos mooing and the thoughts of snakes hiding themselves beneath the sand where my sleeping bag was positioned kept me awake and the times when I fell asleep through exhaustion I was jolted out of sleep by the real noises I thought were imagined. Throughout the night I called Sharif to make sure that he was awake and listening too.

Monday, 10 January

We awoke at 05:30 by the banging of tin lids by Henora! We were washed and breakfasted and were on our way by 06:30.

The vastness of the area and being engulfed by wild-life The silence, tranquillity and therein peace of our surroundings were awesome.

By 10 a.m. we stopped under a large mature tree, which provided a welcomed shade from the relentless heat rays that were pelting down on us.

Water that we had purified in the morning was now almost finished. Henora assured us that we could safely drink directly from the free flowing water of the Zambezi River (as he was doing). However, having seen the animals in the water and witnessed their excretion habits .....we held back. My throat was dry.

The blaze of the sun showed no mercy as we made our way down the great river.

With each stroke of the oar, the canoe propelled forward and the wind rushed by cooling our faces, but still the heat was more, much more than this mild gentle wisp of a breeze was able to handle.

The purified water now completely gone, I timidly dipped my mug into the running water; examining it closely, it looked clear, no smell at all and was cold even ice cold. I glanced ahead and watching Henora reached down scoop up and drank the water; I thought 'now it's my turn to drink'.

By the end of the day our tin mugs was scooping clear mineral enriched water from this great river and loving every drop as the coldness stroked the back of our throats as it found its direct route to our stomachs; along with hats, caps and scarves became our defences against the heat.

Henora adjusted his program to allow us to rest between the hours of 12 and 2 p.m. when the sun was at its most intense. Not yet fully adjusted we had a longer break: and not having slept the night before I now fell asleep and woke again close to 2 p.m.

We set off again; at one point I watched elephants with their young drinking their day's fill from the river that we were in, how wonderful! This was not a zoo, no locking up at night, we were in their territory. Henora told us that the African Elephant was the biggest mammal on earth and that they flapped their ears to cool themselves because the capillaries in the ear was close to the skin surface and blood flow enabled their cooling system to work efficiently.

At 6:30 we arrived on an island and set up camp for the second night. With the now familiar routine everyone, fell in line and did what they needed to do before falling asleep contented but exhausted and with sleep coming to us all very easily we slept like a log.

Tuesday, 11 January

Today our set off time was 06:15; a whole fifteen minutes earlier than yesterday.

Today the river was busy with wild life.

The sun bouncing off its dark unassuming surface occasionally caught us off guard as it glistened back in our eyes. Suddenly Henora stopped paddling allowing him to slow down until he was side by side with the canoe directly behind him, then telling Gwen and Carol its occupants to:

'Get closer to the bank and be quiet.'

His voice was quiet and firm, ensuring that the instructions were followed without question.

This passed swiftly and quietly down the line and immediately acted upon.

Then I saw it!

On the left ahead of us were about six hippopotamus in the water with their young.

As we got closer they ducked under the water but keeping their twelve pairs of eyes just above the water line. Their eyes, being the only visible part above the waterline, of their whole enormous body, turned and watched our every move as we filed pass; it was clear that we were part of their world and that they were the ones granting us permission to travel through it.

We stopped at 11:30 and took shelter under a tree, lunched and slept until 2:30 p.m. then we were away again.

Hippos galore! It was with Henora's skill that we fully engineered our way around them; at times canoeing down the other side of the Zambezi which is closer to Zambia; at other times on our usual side, even taking impromptu breaks to give them time to leave or reposition themselves before our canoes went by in the water.

We began to feel more relaxed and confident when approaching the herds and fell into a well-practiced routine, led by Henora.

Until, that is…

We approached a herd with a very young calf. The mother saw us from a long way off and rather than sink back into the water and watch us with her eyes at water level (like the others had done and we now grew to expect), she stood up on her hind legs. The riverbank to our right had a steep drop leaving us no chance of getting out onto dry land, which would bring its own dangers; we had to pass her.

As we drew closer to the herd, she snorted a pool of air blowing water directly at the canoes. We kept silently paddling as close to the bank as we possibly could and as Henora had signalled for us to do; this action prevents her being able to go under the canoe and tip it upside down.

The mother came down from her hind legs broke free from the rest of the herd and headed directly at our canoes and took the action that we most feared – she dived under the water.

Our arms went into overdrive paddling as fast as we possibly could. She re-emerged out of the water in the middle of the river; realizing that she was not as close to us as she wanted to be, she looked around, bashing the water with a heavy thud sending out an almighty splash with water traveling in all directions, before taking a second dive under the water.

Four of the five canoes had now passed where she might reappear, if she swam in a straight line, but the fifth boat had not yet passed the imaginary line when the hippo re-emerged out of the water raising its angry head and missing them with only a few inches to spare.

We continued to paddle as fast as we could until

she had rejoined the rest of the herd and we were out of her sight.

Henora stopped as soon as it was possible and gave us a de-briefing. It was only then that we realized that he had a shotgun with him. He explained that if any animal is killed there is an investigation; the Hippo behaved in the manner that it did because it was stressed or protecting its young and he, Henora needed to radio the next group behind us to warn them of this.

The ꝑ Rangers and guides are under strict orders to space the tours out evenly to prevent distress to the animals.

Wednesday, 12 January

Our routine set us on our way by 7:30, which was late for us. After about an hour on the river we could see ahead of us where it narrowed and branched into two streams of very low water levels. Looking in the direction of travel we saw a crocodile flashed its tail and ran back onto the riverbank. Crocodiles he had told us could grow to 4-5 metres long and would not have to eat for six months after only one large meal.

Henora stopped the procession telling us we had to get out and pull our canoes since the water was not deep enough. I asked him if he saw what we just witnessed; at this point my stress levels were off the scale; but we all fell in line and got out of our canoes and began to pull it through the shallow water until we all reached the other side of the shallow area when we were able to get back in and continued our journey in less shallow waters.

At this point I felt that my stress levels and blood pressure was set to burst through all my veins in my body (had I been asked to do anything similar in the near future) I wanted to call a taxi and get out of here. But there were no taxis and no other way out other than by canoe!

About another hour went past when Henora stopped abruptly and informed each canoe in turn that we were approaching another herd of hippos!

On hearing this I felt faint but realized that now was not the time to faint. I asked him if there was any other way that I could travel because I had had enough... I was almost prepared to walk! (Yes, foolish I know).

Henora's face gradually expanded into a wide grin before not being able to hold it in any longer he burst into uncontrollable laughter.

We had in fact FINISHED!!!!!!

We made our way up the river bank to camp, where we were allocated a tent and not just mosquito netting. Camp was a large clearing in the woods and still surrounded by wild animals.

Hyenas visited us and we listened to lions roaring in the background. As though taking a short cut a large grey elephant casually wandered into our camp. With images flashing through my mind of this great creature creating havoc in the camp by just a swipe of his trunk or a short gallop in any direction, I began to move away (not knowing where was best to hide).

Scott the trainee guide whose height was approximately 5 feet, stepped forward and stood in front of the almighty elephant and lifting both his extended arms simultaneously (as though he had grown wings and was trying to take off) began to say:

'Shoo, shoo.'

The elephant almost nodding its head and flapping its big ears back and forth as it tried to negotiate itself around Scott.

Each time it went left, Scott would jump his small-framed body left, it tried to go right but Scott would jump to the right, each time lifting and flapping both arms and repeating the;

'Shoo, shoo' noises as though he was ushering out small domestic animal.

The great elephant realizing that there was no other direction in which to travel, with the grace and elegance of a prima ballerina, backed itself out of the camp nodding and flapping its big ears backwards and forwards; once away from the tents, large table and cooking equipment turned its huge body scampering away into the dense woods behind him.

After this show of courage, we gathered around Scott, who said simply:

'He wasn't serious he was just trying his luck.'

'How did you know?' we asked.

'His head and his ears,' he replied.

Dinner was of a very high standard throughout but this evening it was even more special. We went to bed early and rested well after an eventful day.

Thursday, 13 January

We all woke early to the smell of fresh roasted coffee bubbling on the open fire. One by one we crawled out of our tents, washed and dressed, we took a place at the long wooden table.

Today for the first time in three days we did not have our morning wash in cold running river water. We also had proper toilets replacing the need to run into the distance with a biodegradable toilet roll.

Real showers and toilets of a sort were a luxury and much appreciated.

We busied ourselves chopping tomatoes, onions another person sliced the bread whilst Henora and Scott (the elephant shooing person) took charge of the fire to fry bacon, eggs, sausages. Cereals, butter, and milk were placed on the clean table cloth.

It was noticeable that as the aroma of the cooking filled the air more eyes gathered to watch us, in the form of small playful monkeys.

We talked and ate; eagerly re-enacting the bonding experiences of the past few days. The small monkeys were coming closer to us and appeared playful, even at times showing off doing back flips and climbing and jumping from the tall trees which surrounded the camp.

Henora had told us that on the drive back he would redirect Leon the driver to do a slight detour taking us on a safari. We were so excited and grateful to Henora for all his kindness and protection.

I notice that one of the monkeys had picked something from the ground. They continued to jump around and being reassured by Henora that they would not hurt us we left them to play turning back to our conversation. Just at that moment we heard a rustle behind us in the bushes and in unison we all turned around to see what the cause of the noise was. As we turned, in that instant, one monkey rushed forward grabbed a handful of the sliced bread and pounced back knocking over a few utensils on his retreat. We then turned back in the direction of the noisy utensils falling to the ground; to see the cheeky monkey taking his last few steps on the ground before pouncing back into the tree.

The manoeuvre could not have been timed better and executed with expert precision; even the picking up and the throwing of the stone to distract us!

We were advised not to feed the animals. We washed and cleaned and cleared everything away before leaving.

We completed our safari as promised by Henora and returned to the hotel. We later met Henora and had dinner with him.

Thursday, 13 January
Victoria Falls (Mosi Oa-Tunya)

We arrived to witness the awesome power of Mosi oa-Tunya (Smoke that Thunders) on another swelteringly hot day.

The water above the actual Falls appeared deceptively tranquil and flows steadily; until, that is, it hits the ledge creating the Falls by using over 600 million litres of water per minute, then plunges between 85 to 108 metres down and away from the support of the rock-lined floor of the mighty river and into the Indian Ocean.

Liken to a terracotta army, marching forward into battle, those behind the fallen continue to advance forward. Spectators from on high are able to anticipate the inevitable demise of the army but still they march forward. In the same way the power of the litres and litres of water crumbles at the end of the

Falls into a thunderous roar and spitting back sprays as tall as 1650 feet (503 metres) into the air!

The spectators perched on raised platforms and mindful of a slippery end as they tread the waters, becoming drenched in the return shower, sprays or downpours in some places. This constant humidity and watering of the surrounding area has produced unique vegetation not seen elsewhere in the world.

The Falls have the power to draw those wishing to end their existence on this earthly plain and this beautiful spot is chosen by far too many to fly once more as wingless birds into the thunderous mist.

It is said that the Falls are named after Queen Victoria by David Livingston who visited in 1855, hence, the statue of him. However, as Zimbabwe reasserts its rights even this piece of history may become less prominent.

Friday, 14 January

Cuno's Market

Our venture into Cuno's market today saw a vibrant and busy place. Colours bursting at me everywhere that I turned. The stallholders beckoning and smiling for you to approach their stall:

'Come, come my sister.'

'My brother I have waited a long time for you now,' said another to Sharif.

Some stall holders choosing to mount their wares upwards when outwards space became insufficient and in so doing attempts to defy gravity.

We arrived early to see a woman dismounting her wares from her head; and it was a large bundle of second-hand clothes that she dismounted.

This task of transporting large quantities of produce on the head, on this occasion, was achieved by having the outer wrap tied with a firm knot. This meant that the shape now looks like a giant tomato.

The final challenge is to carry the load securely. The load is placed on a small circular ring made of cloth with a hollow centre (like a doughnut). This ring is the first item on the carrier's head that rested on her head and is followed by the load to be carried.

When the women carry such loads their often delicate frame becomes one with the load and sways in time and direction with the load to prevent it falling. In doing this, the carrier manages to adjust the load until it is perfectly centred before setting off.

In the West it is said that ladies at their finishing school can be seen to practice body posture and elegant walking by carrying a much lighter weight on their heads such as a book as they walk up and down and being observed by their mistresses.

Rose, I learnt her name, unpacked her wares of second-hand western clothing and smiles broadly; mainly because she had achieved her aim of travelling from Zambia (next door) from 3 a.m. this morning to arrive in Cuno's market with everything in good shape.

'Hello my sister,' she said to me.

'Hello and what have you got for me today?' I replied.

Having set out her stall she reached for a small plastic stool and sat down; out of another plastic bag she unpacked a beautiful cream crochet bed spread that she was almost finishing. She pointed to another smaller but equally beautiful work already completed and said, 'I can let you have that one.'

I gladly purchased a round crochet table cloth for R50 according to Rose that was with the R10 discount.

The women showed me how to crochet; they allowed me to hold their baby (crossing the baby's palm with silver which I did).

We exchanged addresses and I contributed to her supply of Western clothing for many years.

This was great fun!

The Responsible Employer

On our last evening in Zimbabwe, we agreed to meet a friend who had returned to work on his father's farm; we met at the Sheraton Hotel and he soon joined us for dinner.

Kevin was a Zimbabwean but had lived away for many years while he pursued his career as a body builder in the UK and Sharif and he had a mutual friend.

Although Kevin had stopped actively competing he still took care of his appearance and insisted on only eating protein and vegetables and no desert. We were on holiday so we did not eat the same as Kevin.

In explaining to us how he found resettling in his homeland; Kevin chose to speak of the burden that is placed on anyone who employs staff in Zimbabwe such as farmers.

Kevin clearly did not like that his workers looked to him for their welfare, schooling of their children, housing and their own general health; as well as counsellor (unofficial Magistrate) to his many dedicated and loyal staff and their families, since the state did not take any responsibility.

However, unlike the UK Zimbabwe and many countries around the world do not have a government run social or health network to act as a 'safety net' for those who are unable to be self-sufficient in these areas.

The US is a prime example where the health insurances are often attached to employment and in some cases the employer will go further to discriminate by allocating a certain percentage of health insurance cover, which, is based on the salary on which you are employed; therefore the higher salaries attracting a higher percentage of insurance cover.

This would mean that although working for the same employer not everybody would have the same level of insurance cover.

We left feeling that he still had the better deal being the keeper of penniless, powerless people who only had their person as barter and therefore would never willingly leave him.

SECTION 4

SATURDAY, 15-19 JANUARY

Cape Town to North London

Café Africa

We flew from Victoria Falls airport to Johannesburg taking one hour. A standby return flight ticket was purchased on South African Airways to Cape Town at a cost of £200 each to travel; as we would be returning to the UK via Joburg it was more economical to purchase the return ticket.

The heat greeted us loudly. The taxis waited patiently outside with men in short white jackets standing by their cars.

My visit to the airport toilet found a homely black attendant just sitting there. Customers came and went not even looking at her. I said 'hello' even though we spoke a different language. I searched in my purse and found the R5, which I have just previously changed out from my travellers cheques and gave it to her; we hugged each other and with tears in her eyes as she continued to express what I felt was gratitude.

The taxi driver, with dyed ginger hair charged us R60 to take us from the airport to our destination of the Observatory area.

Once settled, washed and relaxed, we set about to find an authentic South African restaurant. Consulting our guidebook we followed its directions out of the city and into a quieter part of town to seek the African food we longed for.

Feeling relieved to see something indicating that we were in the right place we walked briskly towards the sign protruding out at the side of the restaurant saying: **African Cafe**

Consumed with wonder at what we would find we hurried towards the sign; I thought of what would be on the menu, what would it taste or look like and it is good that at last we would be in the company of Black South Africans like those in the club on the night of New Year's eve and so we went on speculating.

Sharif pushed the door of the restaurant open triggering an immediate rush forward of our host, right there in front of us, dressed from head to toe in a heavily brocaded long brown, red, yellow and green patterned Dashiki (shirt) and pants complete with matching cap, was a tall white man with thin mousy brown hair and slim frame. As we stepped inside he leaned forward and bowed unfolding his long arm to the right in the direction of where he wanted us to sit. Impeccably he handed us a menu and disappeared into the kitchen where we heard excited low whispers and giggles before the door creaked open enough for us to glimpse a black woman dressed equally colourful.

This must be the new multi-racial South Africa? Immediately I felt at ease.

We eat a bounty of wonderfully tasty food before bidding our hosts a good evening.

Sunday, 16 January
Nanny Come Go

We slept late and took a train followed by a leisurely stroll to the waterfront to explore.

The beautiful waterfront lined with shiny boats galore and some whose crew were kitted out in the same colours as their boats added to the splendour. There were white people selling African arts, carving as well as clothes, however; the strangest thing was that the area was devoid of people of colour, except that is for a Nanny.

A family just boarding a boat with their child who was still in arms and requiring a 'nanny' to escort her leaving the mother free to socialise and enjoy herself; the issue was (if there was an issue) the mother could not make up her mind whether she needed the 'nanny' to come on board and travel with the family or not.

'Alraat Kame,' said the mother but as the round faced obedient black woman, who was dressed smartly in her light blue frock with a small white apron on top, took a step forward the mother jumped off the boat shaking her head and saying:

'No, no, we don't need you. You stay!' her voice up turned on the 'stay'.

She grabbed her baby and pounced back on the boat again but this time with her baby upright in **her** arms. To re-enforce and confirm her latest instructions the woman added a shooing motion with her down-turned hand; reminiscence of flicking pest away be it flies or any manner of unwanted bugs.

The mother, turning and talking to the other women already on board the boat and who, I imagined, were able to convince her that she will need help and that it was wise to allow the nanny to come along; because she again jumped off the boat grabbed the arm of the nanny who by now was walking away, turning her once again in the direction of the boat; whilst at the same time forcibly ejecting the chubby child from her firm grip into the arms and onto the shoulder of the nanny. The mother this time led the nanny to the boat where all three at last settled for the excursion.

Monday, 17 January

From Cape Town to the Edgware Road London

We travelled first class by train (which cost R3) into Cape Town. We found an empty compartment and settled opposite each other in the window seats. A young schoolgirl chose to share the same train compartment with us of a not full train.

The air was hot and humid, so the girl of about twelve or thirteen leaned over and opened the window to allow the fresh breeze into the compartment; when she was feeling cooler she leaned over us again and slammed the train window shut.

There was never any eye contact of acknowledgement of our presence, not even 'do you mind' or 'excuse me' nothing.

We looked at each other and smiled.

Oh this is where you all are?

In Zimbabwe we were happy and free with less tension in the air. Since returning to South Africa we noticed the feeling of oppression, rudeness, and exclusions more acutely than the first time that we were last here.

Today we saw more black people than we have ever seen in Cape Town but unlike Zimbabwe, they were doing menial jobs; people sweeping, selling ice cream, newspaper, peanuts, sweets etc. I sensed a feeling of utter desperation but desperation for what? To feed children, buy shoes, pay rent, buy basic second-hand clothes – may be any of the above.

We visited museum and saw the Bushman (how small they appear) and positioned alongside them were displays of prehistoric animals.

We also visited a gallery and saw dramatic displays of the injustice to the Black race by people with Dutch sounding names.

Our final stop for the day was at a street market that was almost closing on Aderley Street.

Here we met a Black South African man sitting behind a white woman on a stall full of carvings. I asked her about the carvings and what she did not know she turned to the gentleman and he would provide her with the answer of which she would then relay to us.

The carvings were so beautiful and well sculptured, shiny and professional that we settled on buying a medium size elephant that would not only travel well but would be able to fit on our shelf in the UK. The woman left with a roll of notes in her hand to get some change and I took the opportunity to speak to the artist directly. He told us that they are not allowed to have a stall in this part of town because of the Pass that they carried. He did not elaborate and looked almost apologetic.

'The woman is a good woman,' he said before adding that she also exports his work abroad and the work of some of his villagers too.

She returned and recognised our accents to be English, which, led her to speak of places we both knew in the UK. To my surprise when in the UK she sells these products in London on a stall in Church Street Market off the Edgware Road! (A place that is not too far from where we lived)!!

Tuesday, 18 January

Exploring Cape Town

We hired a car from Vikings. With the car we were freer to travel where and when we choose and that was a great feeling. Our destination was the wine region of Stellenbosch and what's more we had the whole day to explore till our hearts content!

We travelled along and stopped in the water front town of Llandudno to have a swim; it was fantastic to be in the Indian and the Atlantic Ocean at the same time, experiencing the warmth of the Indian Ocean and the coolness of the other was magical; we could have one foot in Europe and the other in Africa!

We passed beautiful picturesque towns and villages such as Simon's Town and eventually stopping briefly for Sharif to buy a drink.

He returned to the car furious!

The shopkeeper had spoken the first word of his sentence in Afrikaans saying, '… in my language means Black: my dog is Black,' and with that took his money for the drink.

We first drove to parts of Joburg occupied by the 'Coloureds' and saw the hungry eyes of distrust but also sensing that curiosity would win through if given half a chance. So many questions:

'Where did they come from?' 'What do they want?'

'Whose children were they?'

'Are they visiting someone round here?' 'Are they from the government?'

Without any certainty but these are the questions I would be asking and looking into their eyes as we drove slowly, may have been theirs too.

The close 'back to back' wooden houses not dissimilar of Britain in the fifties (although they were made of bricks) was a far cry from the gated tree-lined mansions we passed on the way here.

We drove on, following the R310 and without warning, like a phoenix rising up out of nowhere, there in front and to the sides of us were corrugated zinc shacks, upon shacks and still more corrugated shacks.

Reminiscence of an image on a biblical scale to include the slight hazy mist (only this haze more than likely were from open smoke fires) as far as the eye could see there were corrugated shacks, bordering the area at every 2-300 yards intervals were, never seen before, what appeared like square shaped boxes with rectangle cut out slits on every side in place of windows; these boxes were balanced on metal tripod-type legs that held them high up in the air and above the corrugated roof tops: they looked alien and intimidating in their current position surrounded by a sea of corrugated roofs.

Without warning the stench hit us; even with the windows closed the smell had a way of seeping in and entering into our little private haven of the car, then into our nostrils before contaminating our very being.

With the previously obtained books from the ANC's office I read quickly and read out loud for Sharif to hear, while he drove. KHAYELITSHA Township was the name of this place.

Tried as we did to stop; the motorway rushed us straight on; no lay-bys; no amenities; no signposts acknowledging its existence; nothing!

The elevated motorway ran through the town like the forward lunging of a skilled swordsman's weapon of choice.

Khayelitsha, (meaning New Town) was built under the principal of segregation of the races and rapidly became the second largest black township in South Africa after Soweto (meaning South West East Township). Continued political unrest and attempts at forced relocation attracted more people to the area increasing its population in 1994 to approximately 400,000. Still the area had no running water, no public transport, no public utilities and one doctor for every 30, 000 people.

The vast shanty town whose construct, I imagine, were not dissimilar to others, were of corrugated sheets, bits of off-cut wood, cardboard and anything else to hand at the time of construction.

We looked on in disbelief of what we were seeing in front of our very own eyes.

We exited the motorway and Sharif took a side turning and stopped abruptly: in front of us were a barrier and a sign, which read:

AUTHORISED PERSONNELS ONLY –
Military Base

The majority hosts were forcibly resettled on 'Home Lands', which, although sounding cosy and conjuring up images of white picketed fences and apple pie were nothing more than barren pieces of land without any prospects of jobs, shelter or amenities.

Those who were fortunate enough to find work in Cape Town were compelled to leave the town by 6 p.m. and it is to Khayelitsha where most returned; only to restart their journey again the next day by walking at least two miles for a bus (if they had money for a ticket) to transport them into Cape Town for a 6 or 7 a.m. start to their day. For the domestic workers this start time would be an hour earlier as they would be expected to prepare the house for its occupants to rise; all this in 1994.

We drove until we saw a yellow bus that stopped on the outskirt of the Township and then we drove in its opposite direction towards Khayelitsha.

We drove around the Township pausing as two girls looked on; we continued driving as the 'locals' eyed the car and its passengers suspiciously and curiously yet carried on about their business.

The white four-door car made its way over the muddy tracts and rolled its way down one alleyway. There were stall holders manning their systematically arranged displays of all manner of things from brightly coloured fruits and vegetables to what looked like road kills. Hairdressers, barbers, craft men, bread makers and sellers as well as the young making their way back to school in the afternoon.

The second dirt tract that we turned into saw people turning and looking but this time more quizzically at the car and its occupants. I suddenly became uncomfortable as I realised that we were very vulnerable. The looks and more often glances reminded me of the way the 'Coloureds' appeared to me; and they had it 'good' in comparison to these Township people.

Although, I felt that, the political tensions were almost 'placed on hold' whilst awaiting the forthcoming elections in April; I still felt the volatility and anger of the oppressed.

It crossed my mind that should we be suspected of anything: 'informers' maybe, 'police officers' or anything else in-between we really would be in deep trouble. That was a situation that I did not want to be in.

As safe as it might have been I did not feel at ease or secure enough to climb out of the car. To walk the alleyway and buy, what would have been, more authentic items that I could imagine would have been found here or to talk to the people and hear their stories I later recognized as a missed opportunity. But I was not from here and felt out of my depth in a strange sort of way.

I could not connect (albeit from a car) with people who had only known violence and oppression all their lives. If things went wrong would I know what to say or do to make it right?

We spoke briefly and Sharif turned the car around and left immediately, rejoining at the N2, now travelling away from Stellenbosch our original destination.

Two hitch hikers stood by the curb side we stopped – they got in. They appeared grateful, we could not understand each other but when they reached their destination they indicated to us – we stopped and they got out.

We arrived back at the Koornhoop Manor House in Observatory still shocked. We hugged each other.

In such close proximity to wealth and for a country built mostly on gold we were still in shock. For the next three- four hours our conversation kept returning to what we had both witnessed:

The vastness of the Township; the density; the stench; police in their watch towers; the poverty; babies playing in squalor; grown men and women carrying brush wood on their heads; a roaring fire burning on the roadside and expelling thick black smoke in the air; the dryness of the earth defying even a single blade of grass to grow.

This is what the host population was given of their land.

FINAL THOUGHTS

I find it hard to believe that these experiences happened over twenty years ago.

Before arriving in South Africa we knew that Apartheid (meaning separation or being apart) was well established and upheld by the authorities. I knew from the TV that under Apartheid the races were separated: in education, where they lived and whom they could marry but like most people outside of the regime, my awareness at best could be described as 'fleeting'.

Exploring the Cape, with its red tiled roof and beautiful waterfront and even visiting Table Mountain was a beautiful experience in a beautiful place. However, like the saying goes:

Beauty is only skin deep.

Ultimately if we are judged it is by the way we treat the most vulnerable in our society.

Ken, who we met in Johannesburg, said what most know but dared not admit; that the few lived well but at what price? That is, to be imprisoned in your own home with dogs, gates, and barbed wires.

Apartheid could not be sustained. Its end was speeded up by whites and blacks of all status, beliefs and gender but no one played a bigger part than Mr Nelson Mandela and the ANC.

During our holidays meeting wonderful people like

Ken, Henora and many others will occupy a place in my heart.

Zimbabwe was wonderful, refreshing and we were able to relax. The people were friendly and we enjoyed some of our most terrifying yet most special of times there.

NORTH LONDON AND
WHAT HAPPENED NEXT

When we returned to the UK, it was a bit of an anti-climax as we settled down to the routine of getting up in the dark and returning home in the dark, the cold, the wet and wind and rain.

During our holidays we had seen a lot; got to know each other better; shared our likes and dislikes, fears, joys and had a joint experience that would stay with us forever!

Now it was back to a weekly routine that included cleaning the house on Saturdays, doing our weekly shopping at the supermarket and relaxing in front of the TV, as it was still winter and cold.

One Saturday Sharif suggested that we went for a walk to Harrow-on-the-Hill; he thought it a good distraction and I agreed.

We got in the car and drove to Harrow, got out of the car and he insisted that we went for a walk. I really could not understand this: it was cold and I knew that we had not done any of the things that we needed to do on Saturdays... but anyway, I thought, we are here now, I might as well relax.

Sharif began to kneel down on one knee: presented me with the most beautiful and perfectly formed crystal clear Emerald engagement ring; to represent my birthstone and the month of our

107

wedding! Yes we managed to plan our wedding in five months!!

Everything was just perfect and of course it would continue this way... wouldn't it?

END NOTE

Born 18 July 1918 – 05 December 2013

Total vote cast 19, 726,579

Nelson Mandela 252 seat (12,237, 655 votes)

F. W. de Klerk National Party 82 seats

Mangosuthu Buthelezi, Inkatha freedom party 43 seats.

On April 27, 1994 Nelson Mandela led the ANC to South Africa's first multi-racial election.

He went on to become South Africa's first black President.

October 27, 1917 - 23 April 1993 Johannesburg International Airport, was re named O.R. Tambo International airport in 2006 after the former president of the ANC Oliver Reginald Tambo.